MANCHESTER THEATRES

MANCHESTER THEATRES

Compiled by
Terry Wyke
and
Nigel Rudyard

Bibliography of North West England
Manchester
1994

Bibliography of North West England

This work forms Volume 16 of the former Lancashire Bibliography series.

© 1994
Bibliography of North West England,
North Western Regional Library System,
Manchester Central Library,
St. Peter's Square,
Manchester M2 5PD

Registered Charity No. 519720

ISBN 0 947969 18 7

Computer processing and typesetting by the Bibliography of North West England.

Printed in England by
Manchester Free Press,
Unit E3,
Longford Trading Estate,
Thomas Street,
Stretford,
Manchester M32 0JT.

CONTENTS

FOREWORD

1994 is a year of considerable significance for the Libraries and Theatres Department of Manchester City Council. On 17th July we celebrated the 60th Anniversary of the opening of Central Library. Throughout the year we have been heavily involved in the organisation of Manchester's year as City of Drama. What could be more appropriate than to celebrate both of these events by publishing a brief history of Manchester Theatres based on the substantial Theatre Collection in Central Library?

Manchester is justifiably proud of its theatrical traditions and present status as the premier provincial city for drama. However, we cannot be complacent. Continuing reductions in public expenditure threaten the well-being of the many Manchester theatres necessarily dependent on public subsidy. The City of Drama Board is well aware of the danger that 1995 onwards may seem very flat after the excitements of our special year. What is essential is that we all strive to maintain our theatrical heritage and traditions by continuing to innovate and stimulate local artistic expression. The 1990s require a different approach to the 1950s when the Library Theatre Company was founded but the City Council, Association of Greater Manchester Authorities and North West Arts Boards will surely continue to have a key role if the current mix of private and subsidised theatres is to flourish and provide the range of choice we have rightly become accustomed to. Nor should we forget that this extensive range of theatres and other arts venues contributes so much to the vitality of the City.

It is most fortunate that the North West of England uniquely has a regional bibliography as an integral part of its Regional Library System for co-operation between libraries. This volume is published to celebrate Manchester City of Drama and conforms with the policy of producing special bibliographies as appropriate opportunities arise. I am sure the readers of this book will agree that it provides an excellent introduction to the history of Manchester theatres and hopefully it will inspire some of you to make use of the Theatre Collection housed in the Arts Library.

David Owen
Director of Libraries and Theatres

PART ONE

Surveying Manchester Theatres

Theatre Royal, Spring Gardens.

SURVEYING MANCHESTER THEATRES

'Look' – he pulled the Manchester Guardian from his pocket: it was open at the theatre advertisements page. 'Quay St, Peter St, Oxford St.' The Free Trade Hall is in the centre of these contiguous streets. He began to tap the advertisement columns. 'Eight theatres in three streets, all number one dates – all on your door-step. I don't think you realise what you've got.'

Walter Greenwood, *There Was A Time* [1]

The celebration of the City of Drama in 1994 will stand out as a year of great significance to future historians of the Manchester theatre. The festival's focus in the ten districts of Greater Manchester that it covers has been understandably on the modern, the presentation of live theatre by local, national and international artists and companies, and on the future, in the development of schemes to extend theatre in to different parts of the community. With the exception of a small number of events including the exhibitions organised by the John Rylands University of Manchester Library and the Manchester Central Library, little has been said or written about the theatrical traditions of Manchester.

This study is unashamedly concerned with the history of Manchester theatre. It has three main objectives. Our principal purpose is to draw attention to the items contained in the Manchester Theatre Collection in Manchester Central Library. A listing of the Theatre Collection is provided in the third part of the booklet. Secondly, we have attempted to provide a short history of the principal Manchester theatres. These historical outlines can be found in the second part of the study. Finally, in the light of the material contained in the Theatre Collection and other published historical studies on local theatres we have suggested various themes that need to be explored in order that a fuller history of the city's theatres can be written. These are discussed in the first part of the booklet.

MANCHESTER THEATRE COLLECTION

The central part of the publication consists of a guide to the Manchester Theatre Collection in the form of a listing of the printed and manuscript material in the collection. The Theatre Collection is part of the Arts Library within the Central Library. It should be emphasised that its focus is the City of Manchester, and that with a few exceptions, no attempt is made to include material relating to theatre in the surrounding towns of Lancashire and Cheshire. Material relating to the theatre nationally and in neighbouring communities is part of the general collection of books and periodicals available in the Arts Library. It should also be noted that although the Theatre Collection is the principal collection of theatre material relating to Manchester relevant items can also be found in other sections of the Central Library, in particular in the Local Studies Unit. We have identified items outside the Theatre Collection when their importance warrants it.

Although not formally recognised as a special collection, the library's holdings relating to the city's theatres has been built up since the very beginnings of the public library system in Manchester. Over the years the library has been fortunate in that a number of the Chief Librarians – Charles Sutton, Louis Stanley Jast – and senior library staff shared a deep interest in the local theatre, an interest that was reflected in the acquisition of theatre-related material. After the Second World War the strengths of the library's holdings on local theatres was increasingly acknowledged. The establishment and early researches of a regional group of the Society for Theatre Research underlined the importance and uniqueness of large parts of the holdings [310,348,349]. Around the same time the Manchester Central Library became home to a live theatre, and the responsibilities of the City Librarian were eventually extended to include its supervision. Over the following years the Manchester Theatre Collection, as it was now commonly referred to, was further developed owing to the careful custodianship and considerable knowledge of Sidney Horrocks and Elizabeth Leach. These traditions of preservation, improvement and acquisition have been continued by subsequent librarians.

Theatre Royal, Peter Street in 1897, Victoria's Diamond Jubilee.

At present the Theatre Collection is under the supervision of Jeannette Canavan and Patti Collins. It has continued to grow by selective purchases and by generous donations. The library has also benefited from a long and reciprocal connection with the local theatre world.

The listing of the Manchester Theatre Collection has been arranged into seven broad sections. The first section of the Bibliography covers general reference works, bibliographies and finding aids, beacons that throw a powerful light across what might otherwise remain a half-glimpsed or even undiscovered terrain of historical literature. They are not bedside books but are invaluable in locating and checking information as well as helping to build up bibliographies on particular themes. The list is necessarily selective but, in the light of the enquiries made by researchers into the city's theatres, it includes key authoritative reference works such as the bibliographies compiled by Loewenberg [22] and Cavanagh [8], single-volume encyclopedias [3,11,13] and dictionaries [25] of the theatre.

The second section brings together the main holdings of material relating to individual theatres and theatrical societies in the Theatre Collection. It is arranged alphabetically by the name of the theatre and it includes both printed and manuscript items. This section indicates that the printed and archive material covering individual theatres varies greatly, some theatres (Gaiety, Library, Prince's and the Theatres Royal) are well documented, particularly in the form of playbills and programmes, whilst for others (Horniman, St. James's and Tivoli) the holdings are slight. Pantomime books are well represented in the collection. This section should be the first place that those seeking information on a particular theatre should turn, though other relevant information may be contained in other parts of the listing.

The third section comprises general studies of the Manchester theatre. As is evident from the titles listed, there is a comparatively small number of seriously researched works on the history of the city's theatres. Manchester is not unique in this, though given the long interest shown in the history of Manchester theatres one might have expected a more substantial list of secondary works. In the middle of the nineteenth century John Harland [302] and Richard Procter [344,345], two of Manchester's modern antiquarians, turned their insatiable curiosities towards the Georgian roots of the local theatre. In the Edwardian period, R. J. Broadbent assembled a mass of information about the Manchester theatres covering the years from 1735 to 1845, though unlike his work on Liverpool this was never published.[2] Broadbent's typescript, *Annals of the Manchester Stage*, continues to be an important source for those studying the Georgian and early Victorian theatre [276]. The indexes compiled by the Society for Theatre Research facilitates the use of Brodbent's work. After the Second World War members of the Society for Theatre Research carried out much systematic research into Manchester theatres, some of which, most notably Hodgkinson and Pogson's study, *The Early Manchester Theatre* [306], was published. Rex Pogson also produced what remains the standard account of the Horniman years at the Gaiety [427]. But the much-needed general survey of the theatre in Manchester was not published. Despite the enormous

Prince's Theatre, Oxford Street, c.1910.

4

growth of interest in local and social history only a small number of narrowly focused studies on the Manchester theatres have appeared in more recent years. Apart from printed books, pamphlets and articles this section also identifies a number of manuscript histories of particular theatres. It also includes the small number of survey articles by Elizabeth Leach [318,319] that have long served as the best introductions to the Manchester Theatre Collection.

The fourth section brings together information about individuals involved in the Manchester theatre. Only a small number of detailed biographical studies of individuals connected with Manchester theatre have appeared [391,392,427] though the Theatre Collection does contain a number of important unpublished accounts relating to specific individuals [423]. Unfortunately, there is no systematic listing of the Manchester-related material contained in the numerous biographies of actors, managers and others involved in the theatre. This is a considerable resource and much pertinent information can be found by a careful reading of biographical studies of 'celebrated actors' such as William Dunlap's study of G. F. Cooke[3], which includes accounts of his visits to Manchester. To read the autobiographies of Ben Iden Payne [425] and Basil Dean [387,388] offers perspectives of the Manchester theatre world in the early decades of this century that would be difficult to obtain elsewhere. Much of significance can also be rescued in the observations, anecdotes and gossip in the many published volumes of reminiscences. The recollections of John Coleman, Tom Slater, Whitford Kane and many others can throw light into corners of the local theatre world which would otherwise remain obscure.[4] Equally important but less easy to locate is the evidence contained in unpublished sources including letters and diaries. Neither should one neglect or understate the value of accounts left by those who were merely members of the audience.[5] Students searching for information about individuals connected with the theatre should be aware of the various biographical reference aids in print. The bibliographies by Loewenberg [22] and Cavanagh [8] can be used to identify published biographies and autobiographies. The directory compiled by J. P. Wearing [29] is also a useful starting point for research, providing information in both the general and specialist theatre biographical reference works. Its coverage extends beyond the actor to include lessees, playwrights and critics, and can be particularly helpful in identifying other members of theatrical families. The reference works compiled by George Bryan [5] and Claudia Johnson [19] also help to reduce search costs in this area.

Section V identifies material relating to the activities of local theatre societies and groups. The tradition of amateur theatricals in Manchester is a long one and, with typical Manchester pride, the Manchester Amateur Dramatic Society laid claim to being the oldest and longest-running group in the country [448]. Such societies represented a vibrant part of the culture of their communities, indeed, contributed to the very notion of community, though local historians have been slow to recognise this.[6] In the case of groups such as the Playgoers' Club [458-463] and the

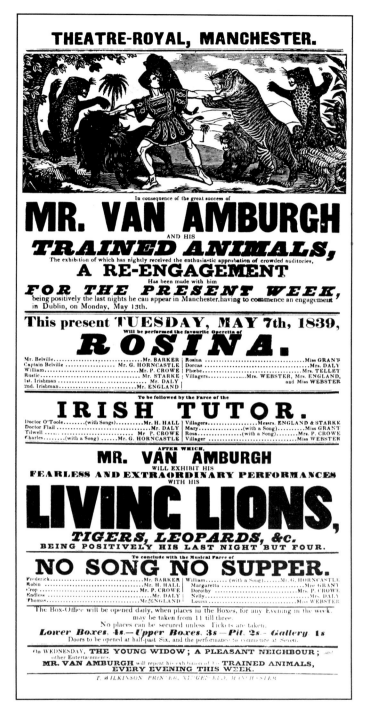

Poster for the Theatre Royal, 1839.

Unnamed Society [474-478] the holdings are substantial. Information on many amateur groups, particularly in the form of newscuttings, is contained in the Theatre Collection, but it should not be assumed that it covers all groups. In fact, the compilation of an accurate census of Manchester's amateur and semi-professional theatrical societies remains to be undertaken, a necessary precondition to any serious research in this important area.

One of the undoubted strengths of the Theatre Collection is its long runs of playbills and programmes for the principal Manchester theatres. The sixth section identifies those not already listed under individual theatres in Section II. The earliest playbill in the collection is dated 1743. Posters and

Poster advertising Macready's Hamlet, 1849.

historian providing answers not only to elementary questions on performers and productions but in their advertisements for restaurants and details of tram times enable the historian to construct a clearer understanding of what was meant by an evening out at the theatre. Playbills also need to be recognised as a major resource for investigating the techniques and work of the local printing industry. Certain programmes contain an unexpected amount of information, for example, the programme marking the 200th production of the Library Theatre includes an invaluable outline of the theatre's origins and development [86]. Careful organization and indexing enables the researcher to consult this part of the collection with comparative ease. Researchers wishing to use playbills and programmes should refer to Elizabeth Leach's survey [319].

As the final section of the listing indicates the Theatre Collection contains a wide range of theatrical periodicals. Specialist theatrical periodicals and magazines represent a rich and, in the case of Manchester, a relatively untapped source for studying the local theatre. Manchester was among the earliest of provincial towns to develop a specialist theatrical press though typically most titles were short-lived, failing to achieve those levels of circulation necessary for survival [513,514,524]. Some titles extended their interest to other entertainments, for example *Stage and Field* [536], or like the *Lancashire Figaro* [510] widened their geographical horizons, in the search for a formula and readership that would reduce the risks of publication. Few publications had the longevity of the *Manchester Programme* [521]. Certain periodicals were specific to a theatre: *The Manchester Observer* was the house-journal of the Theatre Royal [247]; the Opera House also published its own magazine in the inter-war years [121]. Although they vary in size, coverage and type of article, these periodicals and magazines are invaluable to the researcher not merely as a quarry for establishing basic chronologies – dates of performance, appearances of companies – but in providing an entry point into understanding how the theatre was projected and perceived in the community. It should not be forgotten, as editors struggling to keep alive specialist theatrical publications were only too aware, that the activities of the local theatre world were also covered in other general literary and cultural magazines and, of course, in local newspapers. *The Selector* [532], *The Phoenix* [528] and *The Sphinx* [535] are early examples of these magazines. Although this section of the Theatre Collection is strong it is important to note that it does not contain all the theatrical periodicals relating to Manchester. Other titles can be identified by consulting Carl Stratman's excellent guide to theatrical periodicals [27]. Researchers should also note that the library holds runs of the general dramatic and theatrical periodicals – *Drama, Theatre Notebook, Theatre Quarterly* – but for the reasons already mentioned these are not part of the Manchester Theatre Collection.

Although not identified as a separate section in this listing it should be noted that the Manchester Theatre Collection contains a wide range of illustrations, photographs, drawings, architects' plans and other visual material relating to local theatres. Throughout the text we have included illustrations from the collection to underline the range of visual material

other advertising material are less well represented. Theatres with particularly long runs of playbills and programmes include all the Theatres Royal, Prince's Theatre, Queen's Theatre, Palace Theatre, Opera House, Gaiety Theatre and, of course, the Library Theatre. This part of the collection has grown by donation and purchase. It has been strengthened by acquiring programme collections assembled by individual theatregoers including John Evans [482]. Personal scrapbooks such as those belonging to Charles Sutton [497] are rich in local programmes and other theatre-related materials. Playbills and programmes remain an essential source for the theatre

6

available to the researcher. In particular parts of the collection – the Library Theatre – this illustrative material is extensive and would considerably assist the researcher to study, for instance, the staging of plays. Those consulting visual material should note that the Local Studies Unit collection of prints and photographs contains relevant material. Note should also be taken of items such as theatre tickets that have come into the collection. Such ephemera, as theatre historians are aware, can help to fill in gaps in our understanding.[7]

Finally researchers should be aware that over the years the librarians responsible for the Theatre Collection have built up a considerable set of newspaper cuttings files, organized around theatres and theatre societies [332]. These are a major resource particularly when beginning research. They can be supplemented, particularly for biographical research, by the newspaper cuttings held in the library's Local Studies Unit.

This brief outline gives some indication of the range of material in the Theatre Collection. However, as some of the qualifications already made suggest it is important to appreciate the collection's limitations as well as its strengths. The Theatre Collection does not cover all aspects of the theatre in Manchester. There are many types of evidence – prompt books, manuscripts of plays, letterbooks, title deeds and account books – of which there are either none or only a small number of examples in the collection. Although efforts have been made to include relevant articles and essays that have appeared in periodicals or in published collections it should not be assumed that all are to be found in the collection. But even taking into account such obvious gaps it is clear that compared to the local theatre material available for research in many provincial cities this is a wide-ranging and significant collection. It can also be supplemented by the holdings in other Manchester libraries.[8]

MANCHESTER THEATRES

This listing of the Theatre Collection follows a brief history of the principal theatres in Manchester. The individual theatre remains one of the most common entry points into the history

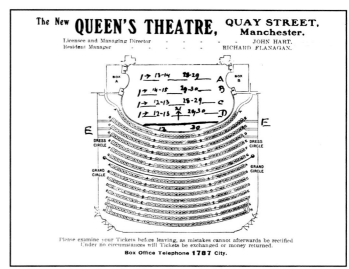

Ticket envelope for the New Queen's Theatre, c.1915.

of local theatre. This section of the booklet builds upon the pioneering and painstaking researches of the North West Group of the Society for Theatre Research. Established in 1949, it produced, among other publications, an invaluable listing of the city's theatres [348]. Later researchers including Susan Hayes [304] and Joyce Knowlson [314-316] have added to our knowledge of individual theatres. In this section we have attempted to provide a thumbnail biography for each of the commercial theatres, though it should be stressed that, even given the research already undertaken, our *factual* knowledge about even some of the longest operating theatres, let alone more transient city venues, remains patchy. This section is arranged alphabetically by the name of the theatre. To avoid duplicating material due to changes in name, a theatre's history is included under its main name, cross-referencing other incarnations to the principal entry.

As for all students of theatre history this exercise has raised challenging issues of definition. What is a theatre? Where did the boundaries of the theatre end and music hall begin? What significance, if any should be given to the world of amateur theatre? We have followed the pragmatic policy adopted by the Theatre Collection which whilst concentrating on the commercial theatre remains sensitive to the fact that other forms of professional and amateur entertainment have a relevance to theatre history. To adopt, for instance, legal criteria, and refer to the types of entertainment licences issued to distinguish between theatres and music hall would be to erect a boundary wall that would immediately cut off from view much that is exciting and essential to an understanding of the local theatre. Thus, in this section we have noted all of the principal commercial theatres that operated within the boundaries of the City of Manchester and, given their significance in the world of popular urban entertainment, identified some of the larger music halls.[9] Had time and space been available, it would have been possible and desirable to have provided a fuller listing of music halls, circuses, exhibition rooms and cinemas in order that the theatre was placed more firmly in the world of commercial entertainment. Neither should the need to identify and classify that vigorous undergrowth of amateur theatrical societies performing in church and school halls, and even rooms in public houses, be forgotten.

Publicity card for Sweet Nell of Old Drury at the Theatre Royal, 1920.

REVIEWING THE FRINGE

Together these two sections will prove useful to all those who have some interest in the history of Manchester theatre. However, in spite of the research already undertaken it is clear that Manchester does not yet possess the historical accounts of the local theatre that it deserves. In recent years despite the enormous interest in local history, and the redrawing of the frontiers of history by social historians and others, little attention has been given to the Manchester theatre. This is partly due to the narrow conceptualization of elite and popular entertainment adopted by historians. On the one hand, general accounts of Manchester's cultural history still perceive it as a musical city, taking as its leitmotif Hallé and the orchestra he established, leaving Manchester's theatrical past as little more than a marginal theme usually summarised by reference to the repertory experiment at the Gaiety Theatre. On the other hand, the thoughtful and careful work that has begun to unravel the cultural complexities of the local music hall has been driven by wider questions about urban working-class culture and, as such, it has not been extended to the theatre.[10] Some new perspectives have ben offered by feminist historians but these remain narrowly focused.[11] Even more surprisingly, theatre historians while acknowledging the value of local studies, have carried out little systematic research into Manchester, though the city's theatres have been used to illuminate more general analyses. At present Manchester's theatrical history remains on, if not beyond, the fringe of most historical accounts. It does not deserve this marginal status.

One Edwardian observer when naming the cultural achievements of Cottonopolis identified the following three: Ford Madox Brown's frescoes in the Town Hall, the John Rylands Library designed by Basil Champneys, and Charles Calvert's Shakespearean revivals.[13] It is a thought-provoking list, not least for the reason that even given the enormous interest in the history of nineteenth-century Manchester there would be a considerable number of students who would have difficulty in identifying Calvert as one of the cultural treasures of Manchester. Yet, a study of Charles Calvert would soon confirm his importance in the cultural world of Manchester [391]. In short, there is a need to undertake further research into the history of Manchester theatres and the individuals who made the theatre a significant social and cultural experience. It is a history that will need to adopt a variety of approaches, particularly those of the social historian, reveal an awareness of the agenda of issues set by recent theatre historians, and consult a range of historical source material that in many instances have not been widely considered by earlier students of Manchester theatres. It is a history that will need to bolt itself firmly to the pervasive social and economic changes that have determined the character of Manchester over the last three hundred years. Above all, in the light of our examination of the printed and manuscript material in the Theatre Collection, it is a history that deserves to be written. Some general lines of further research can be suggested.

In calling for research, it is not suggested that there is no value in pursuing conventional approaches to studying the history of Manchester theatre. Room still exists for more carefully researched historical accounts of both the larger and more permanent halls as well as those smaller and transient venues. There is still only a small number of histories of individual theatres [129]. For many of the smaller theatres, often only known through a single entry in a commercial directory or advertisement in the columns of the local press, even elementary information about site, ownership and repertoire is uncertain. Even the careful work of the Society for Theatre Research should not disguise the fact that key aspects of the town's Georgian theatres remain in an historical twilight area.[14] But in researching the history of specific theatres it is important that they are not seen simply in terms of opening nights, the 'stars' and the visits of London companies, it must view the totality of the theatrical dimension, the theatre as part of a cultural process not a series of unconnected events. It is especially important that greater attention be given to the impact of the underlying economic, social and cultural forces that determined the commercial world of urban popular entertainment. More precise knowledge is required about the impact of those critical forces – changes in free time, the rise of alternative forms of entertainment, shifts in residential patterns, developments in intra-urban transport networks, and rising disposable incomes – when explaining the rise and decline and re-

Publicity card for Richard Flanagan's production of As You Like It, New Queen's Theatre, 1916.

Palace Theatre, 1939 viewed from Oxford Road Station approach.

establishment of the larger city centre theatres. A study of the Library Theatre for example, ought to provide the backbone of a much needed examination of the origins, development and philosophy of the civic theatre movement in Manchester during this century [78-98].

Individual theatres, of course, did not operate in isolation. Victorian Manchester's theatres cannot be discussed without reference to those other commercialised leisure attractions such as botanical gardens, popular concerts and dancing halls. Belle Vue with its ever extending range of attractions, including its spectacular and tremendously popular pyro-dramas [336], is the best remembered of those local entertainments that competed for the pennies and shillings of the leisured classes.[15] Extensive areas of this emerging part of the local economy await discovery. Our local map, for example, of that kaleidoscopic leisure sector of peripatetic travelling shows, exhibitions and dioramas is barely a crude outline. There is no Manchester equivalent of Richard Altick's large-scale survey of this continent of London's entertainment world.[16] Theatres also competed against each other. The opening of new theatres, as John Knowles, the owner of the third Theatre Royal was aware, affected the box office takings of existing ones.[17] When John Hollingshead took over the Gaiety Theatre in 1882, he soon sought an arrangement with the Theatre Royal, in order "to save us both from that wasteful opposition which neither benefits managers nor the public".[18] Whether or not the neigh-

bouring Free Trade Hall was involved in this restriction of competition ought to represent more than a nice irony in any study of the changing economic organisation of local theatres.

Manchester's theatre history cannot be written by simply perambulating Oxford Street and Peter Street. Theatres existed in other parts of the town. Although more difficult to find in the historical record, the penny theatres of Ancoats and Hulme which provided dramatic and musical entertainment for the new urban working classes will need to be part of any critical and balanced historical account of the city's theatres.[19] Even more elusive are those theatres associated with the local fairs.[20] Moving into this century, it should be recalled that this apparently most meteorologically-challenged of all English cities has organised open-air theatre. Less open was the drama work that has gone on behind the walls of local prisons.[21] Neither should the alternative theatre tradition be neglected. Whilst earlier accounts of Manchester's theatres have acknowledged 'rebellions' within the commercial theatre little recognition has been given to those theatre groups whose primary concern was with political and social issues rather than the box office. The development and use of the theatre amongst political groups, ranging from the Independent Labour Party to the co-operative movement, await examination. Manchester, after all, was one of the principal centres in which the Theatre Workshop took root in the inter–war years, Joan Littlewood's arrival in the city

9

Shakespeare lectures, New Theatre, Quay Street, 1913.

adding a new dimension to existing political theatre groups [322].[22] The Theatre of Action and other groups may have exaggerated their power of consciousness raising but, as Anthony Burgess remembered, they showed that the theatre could offer something different in both message and technique to the light and predictable fare served up by conventional companies.[23]

In examining Manchester's theatres it should also be appreciated that they were the venue for more than the presentation of drama. As students of working-class radicalism have made clear, the local theatre was frequently an arena for political demonstrations.[24] In the late eighteenth and early nineteenth centuries when public halls were in short supply theatres provided a natural venue for meetings and other public events: the great Anti-Corn Law bazaar in January 1842 was organised in the Theatre Royal.[25] Theatres were concerned with authority and there is a need to understand how they operated as public spaces and as arenas to legitimise authority. As Chris Waters's study of the attempts by the Palace of Varieties to obtain essential licences reveals, theatres were concerned with issues of power and control and of critique and resistance [354].

As already noted, little serious investigation has been undertaken into the world of amateur theatre in the city. Such research would need to capture not just the activities of innumerable suburban dramatic societies but those groups associated with the churches, university halls of residence, youth clubs, women's institutes and the large city-centre firms and businesses. If the sights of some societies were

raised no further than the school or church hall, others were more ambitious in seeking to develop programmes that blurred the line between amateurism and professionalism. The Unnamed Society and the Green Room proved a cultural force in the city throughout the inter-war years, mounting innovative productions [474-478].[26] In the slums of Ancoats the University Settlement players put on a string of successful productions.[27] Much elementary research is needed into this part of Manchester culture. At the present time there is not even a reliable list of the different venues occupied by those peripatetic amateur and semi-professional companies which, particularly in recent decades under the pressure of inner-city redevelopment, found themselves frequently made homeless, forced to set off once more with all the determination of Pirandello players in search of a new landlord. The records of the British Drama League and the National Operatic and Dramatic Association will be useful in exploring this area. Any history of the Manchester theatre that focuses solely on its purpose-built commercial theatres will fail to capture its essential diversity and vitality, it will be as lopsided as those histories that assume an analysis of the theatre of the West End represents a history of British theatre.

Nevertheless, more needs to be said about the city's well-known theatres, not least about the buildings themselves. Prominent as theatres were in the townscape of Cottonopolis and boasting such architects as Thomas Harrison, Richard Lane, Alfred Darbyshire and Frank Matcham they have been glanced at rather than carefully studied by architectural historians.[28] We still have only a superficial understanding of who built the theatres and who provided the finance.[29] The names of the subscribers who invested in theatres such as the second Theatre Royal have not been discussed in the context of those other Manchester men who financed contemporary cultural buildings such as the Portico Library, Assembly Rooms and the Royal Manchester Institution. Attention also needs to be given to the theatres' interiors as well as their exteriors. In Manchester, little is known about how the internal design and layout of auditoriums changed over the years, even though some local architects – Edward Salomons – were recognised authorities on theatre design.[30] Examination of the interior should not be confined to a technical discussion of size, fire precautions, sight lines and acoustic qualities, but should consider the implications of those changes in the design of auditoriums that throws light on the social history of the community. The refurbishment of Victorian theatres that led to the extension of the stalls into the pit, the provision of ladies' cloakrooms, smoking rooms and, perhaps, that most profound of all changes, the replacement of communal benches by separate tip-up seats (yet another 'invention' that Mancunians laid claim to) need to be considered in the context of that fundamental process of civilising and segregating Victorian society, of instilling social etiquette and discipline.[31] It should come as no surprise that the theatre's attitudes to the sale of alcohol differed from those of the music hall.

Manchester's modern theatres should also not be forgotten. The role, for example, that theatres have played in revitalising old buildings warrants further study. Few more significant local, even national, examples of how to re-use an historically important building can be found than the Royal Exchange, where the installation of a theatre brought new life to what might otherwise have remained a Grade I mausoleum. But attention need not be directed entirely at theatres that were actually built. Much can be learnt about the perceived role of the theatre in the community by exploring those schemes – the Queen's Theatre in the Edwardian period, Beecham's Opera House in Piccadilly Gardens after the First World War and the Regional Arts Centre debated in the 1960s – that never materialised.

Biography offers another line of least resistance in extending our understanding of the theatre. Numerous opportunities exist for studies focused around not just the lives of actors but also the owners, managers, directors, designers and the many others who made up the theatrical community. Certainly more attention needs to be paid to those specialists without whom the theatre would not have been the experience and spectacle that it was. The contribution made by the orchestra and scenery painters to the Victorian theatre is known, yet in Manchester, those who have written about its strong musical and artistic communities have remained virtually silent about how this impacted on the theatre. Neither should we forget those workers – the carpenters, the flymen, propertymen and limelightmen – without whose skills there would have been no performance. Unsurprisingly, little research has been carried out into ancillary services: the theatrical agencies and the costumiers [295,356]. The role played by the theatrical landlady, whose housekeeping skills vied with those of her seaside cousin in the routines of Lancashire comedians, has been scarcely recognised.[32]

Valuable biographical research has been published on theatrical figures such as the Calverts [391], but for the majority of those individuals who worked either on, let alone behind or in front of, the Manchester stage our ignorance is deep. In extending research in to this area, the pitfalls of simply studying the star-names need to be acknowledged, and more effort directed towards examining individuals and groups in the context of the wider theatrical community. There is certainly room for a study of the Manchester actor exploring that agenda of questions set by Michael Baker and Michael Sanderson in their pioneering studies.[33] Little is known about the size, structure, gender, recruitment and organization of the local acting community, and how these changed as a consequence of such well-known developments as the decline of the stock company.[34]

Historians need to be more willing to remove the masks from the ordinary *dramatis personae* of the local and regional theatre worlds when examining their culture. Reading a selection of actors' reminiscences suggests that the public house played a key part in their lives. It was a place to meet and relax, a place to find work and, as Reginald Sackville-West noted, remembering the 'Chester Tour', it could also be a place in which one worked [431]. The Titans, a Manchester theatre club, which enrolled Henry Irving as a member inevitably met in a public house.[35] Some actors might be uncertain about the location of local theatres but the Clarendon, the Salisbury and Cox's Bar were deeply etched on their mental maps. One is left with the strong impression that a temperate actor, like a happy philosopher,

New Theatre (later the Opera House), Quay Street, c.1914.

was a contradiction. How did actors find work? What informal and institutional networks – friendly societies and trade unions – developed to support them, particularly in periods of unemployment or sickness? There is still much to be gleaned from published reminiscences though for more recent times the oral historian has an important contribution to make in recording evidence on the ordinary activities of ordinary individuals who made their livings in the theatre, evidence that must forever remain elusive for earlier generations.

Although the focus of the Theatre Collection is Manchester, the history of the city's theatres should not be analyzed in a geographical vacuum. Hodgkinson and Pogson's work hints at the importance of regional connections when examining the theatre. Connections certainly existed between Manchester theatres and those in other towns in the north west, particularly Liverpool.[36] We should follow the example of that "company of comedians" which in 1761 erected a bridge across the Irwell to ease access to the Riding School in Salford. Such connections remind us that, for instance, those unexplored hierarchies of taste were more complex and subtle than suggested by the hackneyed division that simply separates the metropolis from the provinces. Within the north west there appears to have been a hierarchy of theatres and audiences. Manchester audiences considered themselves to be more sophisticated than those in neighbouring towns.[37] Productions successful in one town did not necessarily do well in another. As Ben Iden Payne recalled after taking one of the Gaiety's flying matinees to Oldham, only to find a very thin audience.

I asked the theatre carpenter if he could account for it. His answer, typically Lancashire in broad dialect, was, 'It's only to be expected in Oudam. You wouldn't get folk to come to a theayter if you could give 'em the Crucifixion with the original cast!'[38]

Developing comparative frameworks can only illuminate our understanding of all aspects of the Manchester theatre world. Town histories of the theatre need to be at the very least regional studies.[39]

But no serious history of Manchester's theatre can ignore London. By the eighteenth century, the capital was already acknowledged as the arbiter of theatrical standards. James Whitley, one of the earliest provincial theatre impresarios, was well aware of the value of bringing London hits – *She Stoops to Conquer* (1773-4) and *The Rivals* (1775) – to Manchester, where audiences were as keen to see London plays as they were to read about metropolitan fashions in the local newspapers. Talented provincial actors were identified and drawn into the theatre world of London. As David Garrick bluntly expressed it when discussing the potential of Elizabeth Farren: "She is much too fine stuff to be worn and soiled at Manchester and Liverpool."[40] Throughout the nineteenth century it remained the cultural centre of the country, even if there was a discernible shift in the economic centre of gravity away from London. Actors might learn their trade in provincial theatres but their status was only confirmed when they moved to and found success in London. It is difficult to overstate the magnetic attraction of London. This has continued into the present century. Theatre groups such as the 69 Theatre Company whose spirit was antagonistic to the idea of the West End theatre, could not resist its financial pull. There was a sense that even those most famous Lancashire dramas premiered by Miss Horniman at the Gaiety were not a true success until they had been anointed by the London critics. Though, even when discussing the provincial significance of Gaiety's productions it is often overlooked that Manchester audiences did not always make the first judgement: *Hindle Wakes* was seen by London audiences some six months before it opened at the Gaiety.

Letter from Richard Flanagan relating to the staging of The Prodigal Son, 1907.

But it was not all one-way traffic from centres of high to low cultural deprivation. Londoners were not entirely starved of Lancashire culture. In one of the more shadowy corners of the metropolitan entertainment world Victorian audiences were treated to the delights of "Mme Pauline and her talented company of female artistes" presenting "Gems of Art representing Pictures from the Manchester Art Galleries . . .".[41] Presumably because such artistic entertainments were concerned more with the physical than the moral elevation of the audience they were not included in those improving activities that Mancunian educators and other citizens publicly applauded.

Surprisingly, theatre historians have had comparatively little to say about the economic organisation and structure of the theatre. Commercialised entertainment was a defining characteristic of urban life. As Celia Fiennes observed of late seventeenth-century Manchester it was a lively town: "musick and danceing and things are very plenty here".[42] Such entertainments grew as the town was transformed into the central city of a great industrial conurbation. Yet, historians of the theatre frequently write as if these changes were merely a backcloth to rather than a central dynamic in understanding change. The scheduling of productions in the eighteenth century had to take into account the calendar of local horse races and cock-fighting.[43] Similarly in the nineteenth century the changing pattern of the working week and holidays considerably shaped the form of theatrical performance. In this century no history of the theatre can be considered complete without a discussion of the impact of not only the cinema and television but also the bingo hall, skating rink and bowling alley. Apart from the often repeated view that these new forms of leisure contributed to a decline in audiences, little is known about the actual impact of these other forms of commercial entertainment. Yet, these relationships may not have been as simple as hypothesised. Television, which along with the cinema has been held responsible for the great haemorrhaging of talent – directors, writers, actors – from the theatre, did not always have that effect. Granada Television's encouragement of drama at the University of Manchester and, less successfully, its promotion of the Stables Theatre project, suggest that causal relationships might not be as simple and linear as asserted. To research such questions adequately will need a much clearer understanding of the economics of the regional leisure sector than is evident in most studies. At present our understanding of the economic impact of the theatre is not much further advanced than when the ever industrious Axon tentatively estimated the annual revenues of theatres and music halls [270].

Considerable research is also needed to unlock the business and managerial methods of those who operated the theatres. In general, theatre histories have given insufficient attention to box-office receipts, yet for lessees the difference between revenues and costs was the central fact of life. What business skills were necessary to operate a theatre? How was capital raised? How could the apparent high risks involved in mounting productions be reduced? Here the fact that our knowledge of the lives, let alone business methods and dealings, of lessees and managers of the stature of Fred Barney Egan, J. Pitt Hardacre and Richard Flanagan, rarely exceeds

Extract from the Gaiety Theatre Share Receipts Book, 1907.

modern version of that ancient drama, "The Miseries of Management", presumably with new acts entitled "The Disappearing Subsidy", "The Elusive Sponsor" and "Managing the Deficit".[46] Although the extant business records of Manchester theatres are incomplete, the Theatre Collection contains financial accounts, leasing agreements and other papers that would prove valuable in beginning to investigate some of these issues. Other types of document can also throw light on important areas of management. Thus the rich collection of playbills and posters prompt questions about publicity, and how this altered over the years. To some observers such developments were as significant as changes in repertoire and acting styles. Louis Hayes' fanciful condemnation of late Victorian theatre advertising methods prompts enough questions to suggest the need for at least one serious study of this overlooked area of theatre history.

Then, too, theatrical advertising was a very modest affair, as compared with the elaborate posters, pictorial and other-wise, which now crowd the walls and the hoardings of our towns and cities. Then a few bills about 18 by 8 inches coarsely printed and pasted on some iron frames scattered throughout the leading avenues to the city, were practically the only public announcements made, or inducements held out to visit the theatres or discover their attractions . . . The old, quiet way of advertising a performance or a play, would be really quite refreshing compared with the coarse, offensive pictorial exhibitions which are now so common. It is no wonder that the enjoyable shilling pit has had to be abolished, in the face of the enormous expenditure which is now considered necessary to draw audiences to the various entertainments.[47]

Business historians who have generally displayed little interest in the theatre should begin to rectify this neglect and look more closely at this sector of the Manchester economy.

Discussion of theatre finances leads to consideration of who actually bought the tickets. Who went to the theatre in Manchester, and why? How socially selective were theatre audiences? Was the theatre one of the few public arenas in which the classes and the masses actually met face to face? How deep into the working classes did the theatre-going habit penetrate? How did the social mix of audiences change over time? What were people's expectations of a night out at the theatre? While historians of Manchester have written about the reverberations of the great migration of servant-keeping families – in Michael Kennedy's phrase "the Cheshire withdrawal" – on the local corridors of power, little has been said about its impact on the audiences of the Theatre Royal and the Prince's. The work of George Wewiora [357] has begun to illuminate some of these areas but in general, we have only the most impressionistic, anecdotal evidence of the social complexion of audiences.[48] James Kay, qualifying his picture of a working class starved of recreational amenities, informed the *Select Committee on Public Walks* in 1833 that "at present the entire labour-ing population of Manchester is without any season of recreation, and is ignorant of all amusements excepting a small proportion that frequents the theatre".[49] But how small, and which theatres did they patronise? In the light of what

that available in their press obituaries is an obvious barrier. The careers of innovative businessmen such as William Henry Broadhead, who built up an important theatre circuit in and around Manchester, have not been fully analyzed. It will only be through careful study of the business careers of lessees like Edward Garcia, whose financial dealings appear to have made him as familiar with the chapters of the bank-ruptcy laws as with the texts of the plays he put on, or David Prince Millar who is reputed to have taken over the Queens Theatre in the 1850s "with a capital consisting of a sixpence and a fourpenny-bit",[44] that the nature of the risks and rewards involved in operating a Victorian theatre will become evident. In researching this aspect of theatre history it is important that attention is given to those who failed not just to those who were successful.

Such studies should also throw light on those processes, presently indistinct, which led to the selection of the 'right' production that matched the tastes of the audience. Critics who complained of frivolous shows usually overlooked the level of risk associated with mounting more serious productions. Thus, as John Knowles knew, one might offer something more thoughtful and cerebral but there was no guarantee that all of one's regular patrons would turn up. There was a cost involved in trying to raise the level of public taste. It was less riskier for the Theatre Royal to serve up "sensational" plays, light-hearted dramas or even equestrian shows in its search for a profit.[45] What was true of nineteenth-century theatre is also the case in the twentieth century where, even leaving on one side the profound changes that have occurred in theatre economics, we remain largely ignorant about theatre finances and the playing out of the

Queuing for tickets: the Palace Theatre, Oxford Road, c.1925.

is known about the economic vulnerability of large sections of the working classes what truth is there in Neville Cardus's view of the years before the First World War that "to go to a theatre was as natural a perquisite of the poor and half-educated as oranges and football matches."[50] Until the second half of this century hard data on age, gender, class and residence is scarce, often only available in that most distressingly created of all evidence, the deaths resulting from a fire or a panic in a theatre. The panic at Ben Lang's Music Hall in 1868 which left over twenty dead (almost all were teenagers working in either Manchester or Salford) and many more injured, allows one to pierce briefly the sociological anonymity of the audience.[51] No history of the Manchester theatre can be considered complete that does not try to look more closely into the broad social categories suggested by the gallery, the stalls and the pit.[52] We need to understand more about the social arithmetic of audiences before we can analyze adequately the algebra of audiences' tastes and enjoyments, of class attitudes and allegiances, and how these helped to shape what was produced on the stage. Questions outnumber answers but significant insights, as George Hauger has suggested, may be gleaned, for example, by a more careful combing of the autobiographies, diaries and letters left by those who visited the theatre.[53]

A further important and largely neglected theme in the history of Manchester's theatre is the role played by the press. The rise and apparently increasing influence of the dramatic critic has been only lightly sketched and, in truth, we know little about the journalists who wrote about the local theatre. The knotty problem of whether theatre critics had the power to influence tastes and ticket sales has not been unpicked. The exception to this is, of course, the *Manchester Guardian* whose theatre critics have been acknowledged as powerful voices in determining contemporary notions of proper theatre. In the mid-Victorian decades the reviews of John Harland and Charles Sever began to set new standards though other local newspapers also hired perceptive reviewers.[54] But it was under C. P. Scott's editorship, that the *Manchester Guardian* acquired its formidable reputation for theatre criticism.[55] Its reviewers were an impressive group of intellectuals and men of letters: Oliver Elton, Alan Monkhouse, C. E. Montague, W. S. Houghton, Harold Brighouse, and G. H. Mair. If theatre scholars remain apprehensive about the concept of a 'Manchester School of Drama', there should be fewer qualifications surrounding the idea of a 'Manchester Guardian School of Drama'. When Ben Iden Payne was trying to persuade Miss Horniman that Manchester rather than Scotland was the place to set up a new theatre, one of the city's cultural assets he identified was the theatre criticism offered in the columns of the *Manchester Guardian*.[56] But such reviewers wrote within a distinct frame of cultural reference, their notices taking the form of essays infused with the higher purposes of the theatre [268, 363, 374]. Thus, although the *Manchester Guardian* provided reviews of the city's larger music halls, significantly these were often left to the newspaper's journalists rather than the established writers. Neville Cardus recalled that one of his early jobs on the paper was to write about the shows at one of the local Palace of Varieties:

. . . a certain Max Erard came to the Manchester Hippodrome. He played an organ in coloured electric light, and he advertised that it weighed eight tons. My notice jumped at the obvious opportunity for satire. He retaliated with a strong letter to the Editor, threatening horse-whipping. A few weeks afterwards he was back at the Manchester Hippodrome, top of the bill – "Return of the Great Max Erard." Mills again sent me to write of him; but as I thought it might seem cheap to go over the same ground, I omitted mention of Erard at all, concentrating on some more or less anonymous first turn of the show. As it happened, Sidebotham was this time taking (that is, editing) the music-hall notices, and I had attended a Monday matinée. Just before six o'clock Sidebotham came into the reporters' room and touched me gently on the arm. "You've not discussed Erard and his organ", he said. I explained that I could add nothing to my notice of a month earlier. "But," persisted Sidebotham, "if you don't mention him again he'll think his threatening letter has dismayed us." He took me below to the Thatched House and stood me the first whisky and soda of my life. It flew to my head, and I went back to my Manchester Hippodrome notice and added, "Max Erard returns this week with his organ. It still weighs eight tons.[57]

No doubt this brought a smile to those who considered themselves "intelligent playgoers" and who probably had never set foot inside the Hippodrome, but such a review underlines the division that separated the serious from the frivolous, by which Scott steered the newspaper. It is doubtful whether such cleverness would have been considered appropriate for a theatre review. But in focusing on Cross Street it should not be forgotten that other newspapers and magazines with different readerships in mind approached the popular theatre more sympathetically, often content to review what was happening on the stage rather than what ought to happen. As the considerable number of theatre periodicals in the Theatre Collection indicates, it would be highly misleading to write a history of the city's theatre press solely from the pages of the *Manchester Guardian*.

In drawing attention to these areas of Manchester's theatre history it is not suggested that what was performed on the Manchester stage was unimportant. In fact the questions surrounding repertoire and acting that form a central part of the writings of modern theatre historians would benefit from being examined by local case studies. A clearer understanding of what productions audiences saw, and how they reacted to them, at the city's theatres is required. Reading some secondary accounts it might be assumed that Manchester audiences were fed almost exclusively on a diet of overcooked London shows and frothy Christmas pantomimes before the arrival of Miss Horniman [280]. Yet, a closer examination of programmes in the Theatre Collection indicates that even at the Gaiety the Manchester-born actor-manager, Harold Neilson, was offering *A Doll's House* and *Enemy of the People* some time before Miss Horniman had left Dublin. *Captain Brassbound's Conversion* was given its first public performance at the Queen's Theatre in 1902, still a time when Shaw's iconoclastic work caused individuals who had only heard about, let alone seen, his plays, to dispatch letters to the press. But in focusing on the 'New Drama' and those productions that would have met with the approval of the Manchester Dramatic Reform Association and the Playgoers' Club [458-463] we should not make the assumption that the more mundane forms of drama, the melodrama and the pantomime, lacked substance and originality.[58]

We are also unsure about how plays were presented. In what ways did the productions put on by provincial companies differ from those in London? It would be revealing, for instance, to trace the shifts in how Shakespeare

Theatrical Management, 1933 (left to right): George Lee, Prince's; J. Hewitt, Palace; W. Taylor, Palace; D. Bush, Palace; F. R. Bolton, Opera House; Fred Brooks, Hippodrome; J. Garley, Hippodrome; F. Madjdany, Opera House. Finnie, Daily Dispatch.

was presented to Manchester audiences over the centuries: from the doctored texts of Colley Cibber through to the modern costume versions. Locally, Charles Calvert became renowned for the historical accuracy of his productions, going to extraordinary lengths in his investigations for costumes and scenery. This included not only dry-as-dust research in the Free Library but fieldwork that in the case of *The Merchant of Venice* took him to Venice from where he returned with a gondola! But even Calvert's concern with the details of the set appeared almost amateurish when contrasted with Richard Flanagan's sumptuous productions, where it was not unusual, indeed, the audience came to expect it, to see grand crowd scenes with lavish and colourful costumes. Sheep, goats and even deer had walk-on parts. One might guess that few other productions of *The Winter's Tale* in the Victorian and Edwardian periods needed to include in their programme notes the acknowledgment: "Bear supplied by Jimmy Lyons, London", even allowing for the animal's presence in the plot.

There is also much to be discovered by a closer reading of those plays put on at the city's theatres. Plays with such intriguing titles as *The Spinner's Dream* and *Manchester Mary; or, The Spirit of the Loom* have been little considered by scholars familiar with the condition of England novel in the early Victorian period.[59] Dramas about factory life may prove just as revealing to an understanding of how the new industrial world was being represented as a study of the period's prose and poetry. As recent work on the Gaiety Theatre demonstrates, a closer reading of the plays can offer broader perspectives on national issues.[60] There is ample scope to add to those "solemn treatises" that Harold Brighouse claimed had already "been written about Manchester plays in the universities of Philadelphia and Pittsburgh."[61] Yet, revealingly, whilst most students of nineteenth-century literature would have little difficulty in compiling a reasonably long list of the region's poets and novelists it would be a more demanding task to compile one of its dramatists.[62] That the names of certain writers will feature on both lists ought not to come as a great surprise.

Above all it is important when discussing the transformations of Manchester theatre that these are set in the context of the wider social, economic and political changes of the society. Thus, to take a theme almost at

Programme for The Sleeping Beauty, Theatre Royal, 1877.

random: although the relationship between the church and the theatre is alluded to in the existing literature there is little attempt to examine it systematically and explain its significance either in terms of local or national religious structures. The broad outline of the shift in attitudes from a period when the church regarded the theatre as a source of moral corruption, barely distinguishable from a brothel, to more recent times when the church has encouraged the establishment of drama groups, and individual clergy could be found on public platforms fighting to keep theatres open, is lightly sketched. Little attention has been given to explaining the factors that led to such shifts in attitude, let alone to the complexities that arise from the different denominational accents involved. Specific issues that would serve as entry points to analyze these wider themes are easy to identify. Thus while the Act of 1775 licensing a playhouse appears as a landmark in the development of the Manchester theatre, apart from some frequently repeated perplexing evidence suggesting both religious opposition and support for the scheme, the character of the local debates surrounding the passage of this legislation remains vague. Similarly, the accusation made by Joseph Aston that it was religiously inspired incendiaries who were responsible for the destruction of the Theatre Royal in 1789 has never been considered thoroughly [302]. Similarly, we have little understanding of the personalities and arguments involved it the periodic outbursts of pamphlets and newspaper correspondence relating to the moral status of the stage during the Victorian period [279,297]. The list of unexplored or underexplored issues could be easily extended.

As studies of the activities of various moral pressure groups that attempted to control people's leisure suggest, the relationships between the churches and the theatre is a rich theme for future researchers. An examination of charity, a related area, might also assist in understanding how the public image of the theatre changed over the centuries. Items in the Theatre Collection suggest a close relationship between Manchester theatres and local charities, presumably because this was recognised as a means by which the theatre world could integrate itself into the respectable culture of the middle classes. Professional and amateur dramatic societies left their mark on the balance sheets of numerous local charities. The Manchester Infirmary was one of the first

Herbert Beerbohm Tree at the Theatre Royal, 1910

charities to benefit from this relationship.[63] By the middle of the nineteenth century a theatrical performance had become yet another way of coaxing money from the wallets and purses of a public which was continually being asked to demonstrate its support of good causes. Even the allegedly tight-fisted John Knowles could be found arranging charity performances (not always in the off-season). Charity could also be mobilised to assist those in the acting community who were in financial need or, in the case of the establishment of a Theatrical Girls' Club in 1890, those considered to be in moral danger.[64] When users of the Theatre Collection explore such themes they might also note that shortly after the Free Library at Campfield was opened, its book fund was boosted by £75, the fruits of an amateur theatrical production at the Theatre Royal.[65]

This guide should not be seen as a celebration of Manchester's theatrical past, for as these brief suggestions indicate our understanding is too often desultory and superficial. In general the analysis offered in existing accounts lack both substance and depth. Enormous opportunities exist for studying the local theatre world. For far too long Manchester's theatre history has gone little further than uncritical proclamations about the Gaiety repertory years, to which, in more recent times has been added complimentary sentiments about the Royal Exchange.[66] In fact, Miss Horniman, like Charles Hallé's role in Manchester's musical history, has served as a screen, throwing into deep shadow rich and complex cultures. One does not want to understate the impact of the Gaiety experiment on the national theatre scene, yet it is clear that even this episode of local theatre history has been selectively studied. Thus for all the plaudits given to Miss Horniman, it is still unclear why, when it came to it, the theatre-going public of Manchester preferred to see King Cinema, rather than Queen Horniman, occupy the throne at the Gaiety. Perhaps one of the unexpected legacies of the City of Drama will be a revival of interest in local theatre history, the abandonment of a tea-card view of Manchester theatre, and the researching and writing of fuller and more contextualised accounts and analyses of the many worlds of Manchester theatre.

OTHER COLLECTIONS

Though the Manchester Theatre Collection will be the natural starting point for such research it should not be forgotten that important material relating to Manchester theatres is held in other repositories, both inside and outside the city. In Manchester itself researchers should be aware of the following collections: **The John Rylands University Library of Manchester** has a number of special collections which relate to theatre and drama in Manchester. The theatre and drama collection contains material of national importance, including the Gaskell Collection. Its printed book collections (held at the Deansgate Building) include Restoration plays, including those of Congreve, Farquhar, Etheridge and Wycherley. Other collections include manuscripts of *The Mountaineers* by George Colman Junior, and *The Man of Pleasure: A Comedy in Two Acts* by a "Gentleman of Manchester". The (Geoffrey) Behrens Collection contains nineteenth-century manuscript material relating to the Theatre

Basil Dean.

Royal, Manchester. Special Printed Book Collections include the Allardyce Nicoll Drama Collection and G. L. Brook Drama Collection, which contain numerous copies of nineteenth-century plays. The library also holds important collections of the papers of two late-Victorian dramatists George Robert Sims (perhaps best known for his ballad "In the Workhouse, Christmas Day") and his frequent collaborator Henry Pettitt. Both collections contain the authors' own typescripts of plays, actors' parts or "sides", incidental orchestral music, and assorted manuscript letters, promotional materials, cuttings etc. The library also holds Henry Irving's own much-revised and annotated promptscript to his 1885 Lyceum spectacle *Faust*. The twentieth-century English Literature Collection contains the Basil Dean Archive. Dean (1888-1978) the actor, manager, stage and film director, had strong connections with Manchester. The Archive contains over 10,000 items, including correspondence – notably with Arnold Bennett and John Galsworthy – and over 30 scrapbooks of press cuttings, playbills, scripts, prompt copies, some 700 programmes, photographs and original costume and set designs. The Horniman Papers and the Annie Horniman Collection both contain considerable information on Miss Horniman's theatrical life. The Horniman Papers contain letters from authors, playwrights and relatives. The collection also con-tains newspaper cuttings, mostly relating to the Gaiety Theatre during the early years this century. Miss Horniman also deposited some 10 volumes of cuttings relating to the history of the Irish National Theatre, Dublin, from 1901. The papers of the playwright Charles Edward Montague cover the period c.1880-1930, and comprise manuscripts of Montague's plays, newspaper cuttings of his articles, reports and reviews in the *Manchester Guardian*, reviews of Montague's plays and his literary correspondence. The papers of Allan Noble Monkhouse cover the period c.1898-1935, and are mainly literary. The collection includes letters relating to Monkhouse's own plays and novels.[67] The Hugh S. Hunt Papers cover the period c.1924-80. Hunt was

Production of Sweet Master William by the Unnamed Society, 1953.

Professor of Drama at Manchester University from 1961-73. His papers include plays, prompt copies of plays, correspondence, programmes, newscuttings and other printed items. The papers of Stephen Joseph are also held. Joseph was Lecturer at the Manchester University Drama Department from 1962-7. The papers cover the period 1951-66 and include material on various theatre productions, theatre designs, plans and photographs, correspondence, programmes and Joseph's writings.

The University of Salford has two major collections which relate to Manchester theatre and drama. The Walter Greenwood Collection is a comprehensive collection of all the author's published works. In addition to *Love on the Dole*, Greenwood also wrote a ten other novels, short stories, plays and an autobiography. There are also proof copies and a complete collection of manuscripts (both of published and unpublished works), correspondence, photographs, and press cuttings with critical reviews of his works. A typescript bibliography of the published works and manuscripts is also available. The collection is accompanied by unpublished dissertations and other critical material. The Stanley Houghton Collection came to light through the research of Paul Mortimer,[68] of the Modern Languages Department. The collection includes an album of photographs of the première production of *Hindle Wakes*, Houghton's most famous play. Its main component is unpublished manuscripts of plays (some previously unknown), and it also contains correspondence, contracts and other photographs. A list is available for both collections. **The Manchester Metropolitan University Library** has a general collection of books and journals to support the teaching of drama, and also material (programmes, posters) relating to the work of the Capitol Theatre.

Chetham's Library has a small miscellaneous collection of material relating to Manchester theatres including a collection of playbills covering local theatres from 1831 to 1846. It also holds the extensive Jennison Collection of material relating to Belle Vue. The **National Museum of Labour History** has no extensive collection relating to local theatres but does hold material

relating to the Unity Theatre. The **Working Class Movement Library** in Salford holds archival and published material relating to the development of the Unity Theatre after the Second World War and on the Theatre of Action and Red Megaphones in the interwar years. The **Co-operative Union Library** has an almost complete run of the *Millgate Monthly* (1905-1953), copies of plays performed by co-operative drama societies, and some playbills. There is no major collection of theatre artifacts in the city's museums but the **Whitworth Art Gallery** has a number of the costumes belonging to Diaghilev's Ballets Russes which performed at the Hippodrome and the Opera House in 1919 and 1928 respectively.

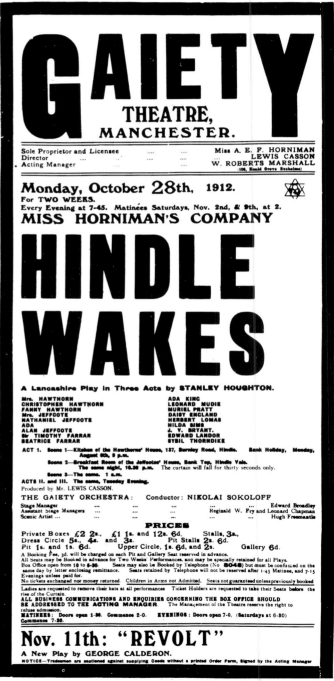

Poster advertising Hindle Wakes at the Gaiety Theatre, 1912.

18

Rehearsal for Oklahoma at the Opera House, 1947.

Researchers should also be aware that a number of the city's theatres possess their own archives though these are not normally available to the public. Researchers wishing to use them should in the first instance write to the theatre to seek permission to consult the archives. The **Royal Exchange Theatre** has a substantial archive including posters, programmes, photographs and cue books. Some material dates back to the 69 Theatre Company. The archive is fully indexed. The archive of the **Palace Theatre** chiefly contains material (posters, programmes, handbills and posters) dating from the re-opening of the theatre in 1981. There are a few ledgers for the Palace Theatre from the early part of the twentieth century. The archive also contains material relating to the **Opera House** since 1984. The **Contact Theatre** has a small archive of posters, leaflets, newspaper cuttings, scripts and miscellaneous publicity material. The **Abraham Moss Centre Theatre** holds a collection of posters and photographs from 1979 onwards. The **Green Room** has a collection of publicity material and brochures relating to performances. The **Free Trade Hall** archives include the diaries of previous managers from the 1950s, and a range of miscellaneous documents including ticket-stubs.

Items concerned with Manchester theatres are also held in collections outside the city. Material is, of course, held in the major national collections. The guide to theatre collections compiled by Diana Howard [17] is a useful starting point when seeking further information on these holdings.

Finally, we hope that this study will be enjoyed by all those who read it, and that it will stimulate discussion and exploration of some of the themes outlined above. As we have suggested, there is a need to advance our understanding of this complex subject if we are to build up sharper and more convincing explanations of the wider relationships that existed between class and culture, authority and leisure, and the material and the mental worlds of Manchester. In the flickering light of our existing knowledge about the role of the theatre in Manchester society it is impossible to say just how important its place will be in future social and cultural histories. What is clear is that it will require more recognition than most historians have given it so far.

Those intending to use the Manchester Theatre Collection should note that every reasonable effort is made to make it accessible, though, understandably, given the rare and delicate nature of some of the material held, restrictions do apply. Researchers, especially those coming from a distance, are advised to contact the Arts Librarian before making their journeys. The Theatre Collection continues to grow, increasing its usefulness. The Arts Library is always pleased to receive donations of relevant theatre material to strengthen this remarkable collection.

We would like to express our thanks to the many people who have assisted in the preparation of this guide, in particular Wendy Broadbent, Jeannette Canavan and Patti Collins of the Arts Group who have helped and allowed us access to the Theatre Collection in the grille. We have also been supported by the staff from the Local Studies Unit. Harry Horton provided information on the development of the Theatre Collection. We are most grateful to David Owen for contributing the foreword. Librarians and archivists in Manchester have been most helpful in providing us with information about their collections and finding the time to answer various queries. Derek Aldcroft, Alan Kidd, David Mayer, Trefor Thomas and Ted Wilson were kind enough to read the manuscript, make valuable suggestions and correct errors. Our thanks also go to the subscribing libraries – public and academic – and our Advisory Committee for their continued support of the Bibliography. I would particularly like to thank the Manchester Metropolitan University for allowing me the time to involve myself in this project.

NOTES

1. Walter Greenwood, *There Was A Time* (1967) quoted in David Ayerst, *Guardian. Biography of a Newspaper* (London: Collins, 1971) p.339.

2. R. J. Broadbent, *Annals of Liverpool Stage from the earliest period to the present time* (Liverpool: Edward Howell, 1908).

3. William Dunlap, *Memoirs of the Life of George Frederick Cooke . . . Composed from personal knowledge and the manuscript journals left by Mr Cooke.* (London, 1813) 2 vols.

4. Thomas Dibdin, *The Reminiscences of Thomas Dibdin* (London: Henry Colborn, 1827) 2 vols; John Taylor, *Autobiography of a Lancashire Lawyer* (Bolton: Daily Chronicle Office, 1883); John Coleman, *Fifty Years of an Actor's Life* (London: Hutchinson, 1904) 2 vols; Tom Slater, *Reminiscences of an Actor's Life* (Bury, 1892); Whitford Kane, *Are We All Met?* (London: E. Mathews & Marrot, 1931); Arthur Croxton, *Crowded Nights and Days: An Unconventional Pageant* (London: Sampson Low, 1934); W. Buchanan Taylor, *Shake The Bottle* (London: Heath Cranton, 1942).

5. For example Louis M. Hayes, *Reminiscences of Manchester and some of its local surroundings from the year 1840* (Manchester, Sherratt & Hughes, 1905) chs.5, 46-51.

6. See for example W. H. Shercliff (ed.), *Wythenshawe. A History of the Townships of Northenden, Northern Etchells and Baguley. Volume I to 1926* (Didsbury: E. J. Morten, 1974) p.271; Derek Deakin (ed.), *Wythenshawe: The Story of a Garden City* (Chichester: Phillimore, 1989) pp.164-5.

7. See John K. Melling, *Discovering Theatrical Ephemera* (Tring: Shire Publications, 1974).

8. See below p.17. It should also be noted that no attempt has been made to identify the playscripts associated with the north west or plays by northern writers. The extensive collection of playscripts held in the Languages and Literature Library should be consulted by researchers interested in this aspect of theatre studies.

9. See "The Round of the Music Halls", *Free Lance*, 25 January 1868, pp.236-7.

10. For instance the work of Peter Bailey especially *Leisure and Class in Victorian England* (London: Routledge & Kegan Paul, 1978) and "Custom, Capital and Culture in the Victorian Music Hall" in R. D. Storch (ed.), *Popular Culture and Custom in Nineteenth-Century England* (London, Croom Helm, 1982).

11. Elaine Aston, "The 'New Woman' at Manchester's Gaiety Theatre" in Viv Gardner and Susan Rutherford (eds.), *The New Woman and her Sisters. Feminism and the Theatre, 1850-1914* (Hemel Hempstead: Harvester Press, 1992). See also J. Holledge, *Innocent Flowers. Women in the Edwardian Theatre* (London, Virago, 1981) and Sheila Stowell, *A Stage of their Own. Feminist Playwrights of the Suffrage Era* (Manchester: Manchester University Press, 1992).

12. For example in George Rowell, *The Victorian Theatre 1792-1914. A Survey* (Cambridge: Cambridge University Press, 1978) pp.138-40. But see also George Rowell and Anthony Jackson, *The Repertory Movement. A History of Regional Theatre in Britain* (Cambridge: Cambridge University Press, 1984).

13. Edward Abbott Parry, *What the Judge Saw being Twenty-five years in Manchester by one who has done it* (London: John Murray, 1912) p.278.

14. "Manchester's First Theatre: A Report of the North-West Regional Group of the Society for Theatre Research", *Manchester Review*, 7 (1955) pp.175-91.

15. Robert Nicholls, *Looking Back at Belle Vue* (Altrincham: Willow Publishing, 1989).

16. Richard D. Altick, *The Shows of London* (Harvard University Press: Cambridge, Mass, 1978).

17. See Knowle's evidence to the *Select Committee on Theatrical Licences and Regulations* PP 1866 (373) Vol XVI Qs.6122-6409.

18. See address "To The Manchester Public" in Prince's Theatre Programme (Performance of Madame Ristori as Lady Macbeth), 6 November 1882.

19. See Angus Bethune Reach, *Manchester and the Textile Districts in 1849.* Edited by Chris Aspin (Helmshore Local History Society, 1972) pp.57-62.

20. See Derek Brumhead and Terry Wyke, *A Walk Round Castlefield* (Manchester: Manchester Polytechnic, 1989) p.27.

21. Judy Meewezen, "Playing for Time", *Artful Reporter* October, 1990.

22. See Ewan MacColl, "Theatre of Action, Manchester" in Raphael Samuel, Ewan MacColl and Stuart Cosgrove (eds.), *Theatres of the Left 1880-1935. Workers' Theatre Movements in Britain and America* (London: Routledge & Kegan Paul,1985) pp.205-55; Ewan MacColl, *Journeyman. An Autobiography* (London: Sidgwick & Jackson, 1990) pp.169-70, 206-17; Howard Goorney, *The Theatre Workshop Story* (London: Eyre Methuen, 1981).

23. Anthony Burgess, *Little Wilson and Big God being the first part of the confessions of Anthony Burgess* (Heinnemann: London, 1987) pp. 180-1.

24. The account of Henry Hunt's reception at the Theatre Royal in 1891 recalled in Sam Bamford, *Passages in the Life of a Radical* (Oxford: Oxford University Press, 1987) pp.126-30 is possibly the best known incident in Manchester.

25. J. T. Slugg, *Reminiscences of Manchester Fifty Years Ago* (Manchester: J. E. Cornish,1881) pp.313-14.

26. Although for the purposes of this study it on the wrong side of the city boundary attention should also be given to the Stockport Garrick Society: see the *Garrick Story 1901-1951. The History of 50 Years of Play Production* (Stockport: Garrick Society, 1951).

27. M. D. Stocks, *Fifty Years in Every Street. The Story of the Manchester University Settlement* (Manchester: Manchester University Press, 1945) pp.73-4.

28. Theatres receive only passing attention in Cecil Stewart, *The Stones of Manchester* (London: Edward Arnold, 1956) p.18, 105-6 and J. Archer (ed.), *Art and Architecture in Victorian Manchester* (Manchester: Manchester University Press, 1985).

29. C.W. Chalkin, "Capital Expenditure on Building for Cultural Purposes in Provincial England 1730-1830", *Business History* 22(1980) 51-70 is essential reading on this aspect of theatre history.

30. Edward Salomons, "Description of the Alexandra Theatre of Liverpool, and on the construction of Theatres generally", *Royal Institute of British Architects Proceedings,* (1871) p.x. Victor Glasstone, *Victorian and Edwardian Theatres: An Architectural and Social Survey* (London: Thames and Hudson, 1975).

31. See for example observations in "At the Theatre of Royalty", *Free Lance*, 28 March 1868 p.105; "At the Play", *Free Lance*, 6 November 1869 p.354.

32. Manuscript material for Manchester is scarce but the Lancashire Record Office possesses the Visitors' Book (1901-1908) of Mrs Robinson, a Burnley theatrical landlady. Landladies feature in a number of autobiographies and reminiscences left by actors. See for example Gracie fields, *Sing As We Go. The Autobiography of Gracie Fields* (London: Frederick Muller, 1960). The young Charlie Chaplin found himself giving evidence in court at Stockport following an assault on the landlady who ran the digs he was staying in at Ashton-under-Lyne: see David Robinson, *Chaplin. His Life and Art* (London: Collins, 1985) pp.49-50.

33. Michael Baker, *The Rise of the Victorian Actor* (London: Croom Helm, 1978) and Michael Sanderson, *From Irving to Olivier. A Social History of the Acting Profession in England 1880-1983* (London: Athlone, 1984).

34. In spite of the difficulties arising from the changes in classification, the occupational data from the national census is an obvious starting point for such research. In the 1891 Census Manchester recorded the largest number of actors in Lancashire: Male, 117; female, 156. Though a more precise estimate of the size and composition of the theatrical community would need to take into account those persons recorded in other categories – Theatre Services, Performers and Showmen – of the census. See *Census of England and Wales*, PP 1893 [7058] III p.368.

35. Laurence Irving, *Henry Irving. The Actor and his World* (Columbus Books: London, 1989 edition), p.104.

36. See Hodgkinson, J. L. *Early Manchester Theatre*, p.76; on Calvert's influence on Saker's Shakespearean revivals at the Alexandra Theatre, Liverpool, see Russell Jackson, "Shakespeare in Liverpool" *Theatre Notebook*, 32 (1978) p.103; on Gaiety and Liverpool see Grace W. Goldie, *The Liverpool Repertory Theatre 1911-1934* (Liverpool University Press, 1935) ch.2, pp.172-3.

37. When Adelaie Ristori's famous Lady Macbeth was mocked by the gallery in a Manchester theatre, a Mancunian correspondent in the press apologised, blaming the "boors from Chowbent". Needless to say the cultured citizens of Chowbent – living in a community "so civilized that it possessed a Town Hall" – did not remain silent. See Charles L. Graves, *Mr. Punch's History of Modern England* (London: Cassell, 1921) Vol.2, pp.283-4 n.1.

38. Ben Iden Payne, *Life in a Wooden O*, p.93.

39. Recent studies include Jane Greaves, *Oldham Theatres* (Oldham: Oldham Art Galleries and Museums, 1977); Tony Flynn, *The History of Eccles Theatres and Cinemas* (Manchester: Neil Richardson, 1986); A.G. Betjemann, *The Grand Theatre, Lancaster. Two Centuries of Entertainment* (Lancaster: Centre for North-West Regional Studies,1982); Robert Poole, *Popular Leisure and the Music Hall in Nineteenth-Century Bolton* (Lancaster:Centre for North-West Regional Studies, 1982); David Owen, *A History of the Theatres and Cinemas of Tameside* (Manchester: Neil Richardson, 1985); James Carter, *Oldham Coliseum Theatre. The First Hundred Years* (Oldham: Oldham Leisure Services, 1986); Margaret Eddershaw, "Grand Fashionable Nights". Kendal Theatre 1575-1985. (Lancaster: Centre for North-West Regional Studies, 1989).

40. R. J. Broadbent, *op. cit.* p.63.

41. R. D. Altick, *The Shows of London* p.349.

42. Hodgkinson and Pogson, *op.cit.*, p. 7.

43. Hodgkinson and Pogson, *op.cit.*, pp.21-24, 31.

44. John Evans, "Reminiscences of the Stage in Manchester", *Papers of the Manchester Literary Club*, 6 (1880) p.291.

45. Knowles evidence to *Select Committee on Theatrical Licences and Regulations* PP 1866 (373) Vol.XVI Qs.6245-6255.

46. *The Miseries of Management* was a short-lived Manchester theatrical journal published in 1805.

47. Louis M. Hayes, *op. cit.* pp.246-7.

48. George Wewiora, "Manchester Theatre Audiences, 1807-1844", Unpublished M.A., University of Manchester, 1974; and "Manchester Music Hall Audiences in the 1880s", *Manchester Review* 12 (1973) pp.124-8.

49. *Select Committee on Public Walks* PP 1833 (448) Vol.15 p.4, 66.

50. Neville Cardus, *Second Innings* (London: Collins, 1950) p.192.

51. See analysis in Dagmar Hoher, "The Composition of Music Hall Audiences, 1850-1900" in Peter Bailey (ed.) *Music Hall. The Business of Pleasure* (Milton Keynes, Open University Press, 1986).

52. See also Rex Pogson's assertion on the working classes attending the Gaiety's plays, *Miss Horniman and the Gaiety Theatre* (London: Rockliff, 1952) p.192.

53. George Hauger, "Neglected Sources of Nineteenth-Century Theatre History", *Theatre Notebook*, 46 (1992) pp.41-7. W. A. Munford, *Edward Edwards 1812-1886: Portrait of a Librarian* (London: Library Association, 1963) p.99, 119. Compare the recollections of visiting the pantomime in R. Roberts, *A Ragged Schooling* (Manchester: Manchester University Press, 1976) pp.49-59 and N. Cardus, *Second Innings* (London: Collins, 1950) ch.2.

54. The Manchester novelist, Geraldine Jewsbury reviewed for the *Manchester Examiner*, see Susan Howe, *Geraldine Jewsbury. Her Life and Errors.* (London, 1935) p.70.

55. On Scott and the theatre see J. L. Hammond, *C. P. Scott of the Manchester Guardian* (London: G. Bell and Sons, 1934) pp.54-6. Scott was called in to settle the quarrel that finally brought about the separation of Miss Horniman from the Abbey Theatre, see Hugh Hunt, *The Abbey. Ireland's National Theatre 1904-1978* (New York: Columbia University Press, 1979) p.91.

56. Ben Iden Payne, *op.cit.*, p.79.

57. Neville Cardus, *Autobiography* (London: Collins, 1947) pp.104-5.

58. See H. Brighouse, *What I Have Had. Chapters in Autobiography* (London: Harrap, 1953) pp.28-9.

59. J. Evans, "Reminiscences of the Stage in Manchester" *Papers of the Manchester Literary Club*, 4 (1878) p.230; G. E. Wewiora, "J. T. Haines in Manchester, 1828-29", *Theatre Notebook*, 27 (1973) p.93. Sally Vernon, "Trouble up at T'Mill: The Rise and Decline of the Factory Play in the 1830s and 1840s", *Victorian Studies*, 20 (1977) 117-39 is an important exception to the general neglect evident in this area.

60. See Elaine Aston, *op.cit.*

61. H. Brighouse, "The Manchester Drama", *Papers of the Manchester Literary Club*, 43 (1917) p.82

62. A useful starting point is E. Romaine Callender, "Lancashire Dramatic Authors", *Papers of the Manchester Literary Club*, 6 (1880) pp.203-18.

63. Hodgkinson and Pogson, *op.cit.*, p.27, 29, 66 and see also G. B. Hindle, *Provision for the Relief of the Poor in Manchester 1754-1826* (Manchester: Chetham Society, 1975) p.96, 100, 118.

64. See Tracy C. Davis, "Victorian Charity and Self-Help for Women Performers", *Theatre Notebook*, 41 (1987) pp.114-27.

65. A. Redford and I. Russell, *History of Local Government in Manchester.* (London: Longmans, Green & Company, 1940) Vol.2, p.228 n.1.

66. Brian Redhead, *Manchester: A Celebration.* (London: Andre Deutsch, 1993) pp.84-5.

67. H. C. Vaughan, "The Dramatic Work of Allan Monkhouse" Unpublished M.A. Thesis, Cardiff, University of Wales, 1949.

68. P. Mortimer, "The life and literary career of W. Stanley Houghton, 1881-1913" Unpublished Ph.D., University of Salford, 1984; "W. Stanley Houghton: An Introduction and a Bibliography", *Modern Drama*, 28 (1985).

PART TWO

Manchester Theatres: A Brief History

Manchester's Theatreland: Peter Street showing the Theatre Royal and Free Trade Hall (centre) and Comedy Theatre (right).

MANCHESTER THEATRES: A BRIEF HISTORY

ABRAHAM MOSS CENTRE THEATRE

Cleveland Road, Crumpsall

Opened: 1975

Named after a former Manchester Lord Mayor, the Abraham Moss Centre Theatre seats approximately 250. It is situated in the North Manchester College and is run under the aegis of the Manchester Education Committee. Although principally a college theatre serving the north Manchester area, it was considerably modernized in the mid-1980s with a view to expanding the range of regular performances to include small professional touring companies.

As a part of the new generation of community theatres, the aims and philosophy of the theatre are diverse and cosmopolitan. Rehearsal rooms and recording studios provide facilities for amateur dramatic societies, dance groups and musicians, along with cinematic equipment for the use of film societies. The theatre also reaches out into the community by encouraging ethnic groups to produce plays with special relevance to the varied cultural heritage of the north Manchester area.

ALEXANDRA MUSIC HALL

Peter Street

Opened: 1865 as the Alexandra Music Hall
Renamed: 1879 as the Folly Theatre of Varieties
Renamed: 1897 as the Tivoli
Closed: 1921

The Alexandra Music Hall, commonly known as the "Alec", was one of the first generation of specialist music halls in Manchester. Situated in a converted Methodist chapel on Peter Street it was opened as a place of entertainment on 18th November 1865. The galleries retained their chapel-like appearance though the atmosphere was far from ecclesiastical, especially in the 'Refec' sited in the basement – the original location of the chapel's Sunday School. The upper gallery was known as the "Royal Fourpenny", or "the Gods", where enthusiastic Saturday-night patrons were more likely to be interested in heckling and throwing fruit at the actors rather than being passively entertained. Seats in the fashionable lower tier cost a shilling or more. The pit was where the working man and his sweetheart were likely to be found, the hard seats costing sixpence.

The entertainment itself was recalled by one observer as "not being overdone, either in quantity or quality". Performances typically consisted of seven turns – six variety acts and one star turn. Variety was the keynote. Assorted acts included ballet, "lion comique", "dashing serio-comics", "charming sisters", acrobats and sundry entertainers. The Irish comedian appears to have been a regular favourite. Of these types of performers, the serio-comic and the lion-comique were clearly losing popularity with the audiences of the 1870s. The lion-comique was essentially a comic singer and impressionist who relied upon the audience's endless repetition of chorus lines – "seeving" – to spin out his act. He was also known to engage in "spelling bees"- comical spelling contests where the comedian put members of the audience to the test. Not generally renowned for his command of the English language, he relied on the contestants to correct his pronunciation! A closely related act was the "dashing serio-comic", a type of female singer one disconsolate contemporary condemned as

. . . one who reared her head unblushingly. Her figure was her only hope. Her voice was a terrible, high pitched, rasping screech, and she had one wooden movement of the arms by which she confidently intended to represent every emotion of the human breast, from joy to despair. Surely she will pass away unregretted, and the stage that knew her once will know her no more.

It is, perhaps, not surprising that the decline in popularity of such acts was linked with the Alec's own decline, although it continued to be regarded as one of the city's most popular music halls during the 1870s.

The building was taken over by Edward Garcia and reopened as the Folly Theatre of Varieties on 3rd November 1879. The entertainment was in a similar vein to that offered

The Folly Theatre, Peter Street, c.1890.

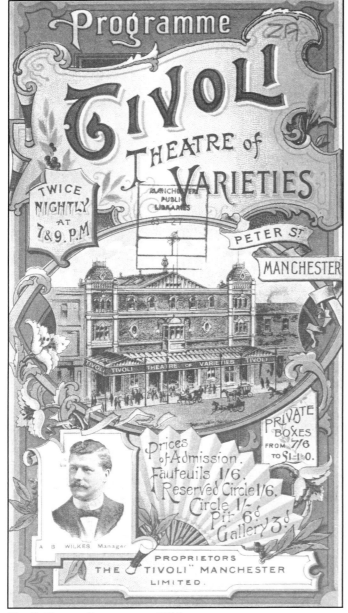

Tivoli Theatre Programme, 1906.

at the "Alec", although Garcia had at least altered and redecorated the theatre. Seating 800, admission cost typically sixpence for the gallery, pit one shilling, Grand Lounge two shillings, private boxes from 10s 6d. Drinks cost 4d for a glass of port wine, 3d for a bottle of lager beer, and cigars were priced between 2d and 6d. Not only was the "Refectory" retained, but also the services of endless "dashing serio-comics" and artistes like "Mephisto, the Man Snake", "Mr W. Salman, the Demon Trick Bicyclist" and "The Veveys – Little Lillie and Her Singing Poodle". Better known acts included Vesta Tilley "the London Idol! singing a new budget of songs", J.W. Hall "the great eccentric comedian", and Little Tich "the quaint comedian".

A new chapter in the entertainment history of the building began when it reopened as The Tivoli on 6th December 1897. The "Tiv" operated essentially as a variety theatre and over the years its audiences were entertained by performers whose names would feature prominently in any Who's Who

of the British music hall. The theatre's fortunes declined during and after the First World War particularly given the growing competition from the cinema. Its last live show was in October 1921. By the end of the year the building was refurbished and back in business as the Winter Gardens cinema. The building was severely damaged by fire on New Years Day, 1927, and eventually demolished in February 1936.

ALHAMBRA THEATRE

Ashton Old Road, Higher Openshaw

Opened: c.1910

The Alhambra Theatre, Higher Openshaw.

The original Alhambra Theatre, opened around 1910, was part of the H. D. Moorhouse Circuit. It appears to have had a rather chequered career as a music hall, and was one of the early examples of cinema adaptation, initially showing silent films by the First World War, and later being fully converted to "talkies". The original Picture Palace was entered from Bank Street, and was situated on the first floor, but the building continued to be used as a theatre for some time. This part of the building subsequently became a dance hall and later, a sporting club.

ALKAZAR THEATRE OF VARIETIES

See Bridgewater Music Hall.

AMPHITHEATRE

Chatham Street

fl. 1797-1806

Apart from advertisements in local newspapers, little is known about this theatre, although it is thought to be one of the many temporary structures which existed in Manchester at the turn of the century. The theatre presented primarily circus performances, and it is known that the famous equestrian, Andrew Ducrow, performed there in the early 1800s.

APOLLO THEATRE

Ardwick Green

Opened: 1938

The Apollo Theatre opened in 1938, showing a George Formby film, and its 2,600-seater auditorium made it one of the largest and most advanced cinemas in the north west.

Extensive modernization in the late 1970s enabled the Apollo to expand its range of stage performances, reflecting a conscious decision to move the cinema into mainstream and variety entertainment. This represented a noteworthy pattern of development, diversifying away from the cinema towards live entertainment at a time when the Opera House and the Palace Theatre were struggling for survival. As such it presents a mirror image of many Manchester theatres that were converted to cinemas from the early years of the twentieth century. Much of its recent success is attributable to the popular and varied nature of the entertainment on offer – pantomime, comedy and film presentations supplement the Apollo's role as one of the city's foremost venues for popular and rock bands.

ARDWICK GREEN EMPIRE

See Empire, Ardwick Green.

AUSTRALIAN MUSIC HALL

Bridge Street

fl. 1866-1868

Little is known about this theatre, which was situated on Bridge Street, Manchester, according to the city directories for these years.

BRADBURY'S AMPHITHEATRE

See Theatre Royal, Spring Gardens.

THE BRICKHOUSE

See University Theatre.

BRIDGEWATER MUSIC HALL

Higher Cambridge Street, Chorlton-on-Medlock

Opened: c.1880 as the Bridgewater
Renamed: 1887 as the Alhambra
Renamed: 1894 as the Alkazar
Renamed: 1895 as the Empire Theatre, later Bridgewater Music Hall, then Bridgewater Chapel or Mission Hall

By all accounts, the Bridgewater Music Hall has had a chequered history. Built around 1880, this small theatre was typical of the many pocket theatres or "penny gaffs" opened in early Victorian Manchester. The theatre itself was tiny, less than 50 feet deep by some 42 feet wide. The stage itself was proportionally large, measuring 17 by 10 feet. The

Remains of the interior of the Bridgewater Music Hall, showing cast iron work.

whole building was only slightly larger than two semi-detached houses.

Its unique nature was not just due to its size. It had a distinctive horseshoe gallery, intricately decorated with a cast iron balcony which stood twelve feet above the ground floor, embellished in art nouveau scrollwork. The theatre was said to be capable of seating around 750 people.

Its history as a place of entertainment was complex, changes in ownership and management resulting in a number of changes of name: it became the Alhambra in 1887, the Alkazar Theatre of Varieties in 1894 and the Empire Theatre in 1895. But the theatre struggled to find the correct formula of entertainment at the correct price and in the early 1900s, it found a different audience as the Bridgewater Chapel or City Mission. In 1910, the building was converted into a boxing stadium, or "blood tub", which was opened by Jack Smith, a former wrestler.

But neither did this venture succeed and in 1914 the building was converted in the great Edwardian cinema boom that re-defined popular entertainment in Manchester. The Bridgewater Electric Picture Palace, known locally as the "Bug-hut" or "Flecky Parlour", remained a cinema until the building was taken over by a company of shopfitters, Templeman Ltd. In spite of these changes, the fundamental structure of the theatre remained intact. These architectural features made it a subject of fervent debate when in the 1970s it was acquired by Manchester Corporation on behalf of Manchester Polytechnic. Sadly, vandalism left this Grade II listed building prone to further damage. Sections of the cast-iron railing from the small upper gallery were salvaged and rebuilt into a corridor linking the Athenaeum Gallery to the City Art Gallery. A larger section of this railing has been incorporated into the Theatre Museum in London's Covent Garden.

BROADHEAD THEATRE CIRCUIT

The founder of the circuit was William Henry Broadhead (1847-1930), originally a Blackpool-based businessman who also ran a swimming bath in Blackpool and ticket writing and sign writing businesses in Manchester. Broadhead established seventeen places of entertainment in Lancashire, which included the following Manchester theatres: Royal Osborne Theatre, Oldham Road; Metropole Theatre, Ashton Old Road, Openshaw; Hulme Hippodrome (later Junction), Warwick Street; Grand Junction (later Hippodrome), Preston Street, Hulme; Queen's Park Hippodrome, Turkey Lane, Harpurhey and the King's Theatre, Stockport Road, Longsight (see separate entries for these theatres).

The "Bread and Butter Circuit", as it was known to the professionals, established a good standard of entertainment, typical admission being 2d, 4d, 6d and 9d. Part of Broadhead's managerial policy was to equip all the theatres in the circuit with their own electric generating plants. The theatres themselves were built to a good architectural standard, usually costing between £9,000-£11,000 to erect. At the height of his powers, Broadhead controlled some thirty theatres, cinemas and dance halls in Manchester, Liverpool, Preston and Eccles. He was later offered, and refused, £250,000 for the Circuit.

The Broadhead Repertory Players performed across the Circuit, presenting plays with popular appeal. Broadhead and his sons, William and Percy, were generally good judges of what Manchester audiences wanted. The young Gracie Fields made an appearance at the tender age of seventeen at Hulme Hippodrome in the revue, *Yes I Think So*.

The two Hulme theatres were joined by an arcade, and it was from the adjoining offices that Broadhead and his sons ran their theatrical empire. Broadhead's son, Percy, later became a theatre manager in his own right, acquiring the Royal Hippodrome in Salford and Palace Theatre, Preston after his father's death in 1930.

Part of the success of the dramatic side of the Broadhead Theatre Circuit lay with the generally high standard of acting achieved by the company. Actors recruited by Percy B. Broadhead to the Broadhead Repertory Players included Paul Neville, Lewis Nanton, Edith Gregory, Madge Trevelyan, Ethel Bracewell and Lilian Travis. The work was exacting and hard as shows were performed twice nightly.

After 1930, the Circuit continued on a smaller scale, centred around The Playhouse (Warwick Street) giving repertory performances and the Hulme Hippodrome (Preston Street) which concentrated on variety.

See also Royal Osborne Theatre, Metropole Theatre, Hulme Hippodromes, Queen's Park Hippodrome, King's Theatre.

◄ *Advertisement for Broadhead Theatres in Manchester and Salford, 1908.*

CAPITOL THEATRE

School Lane, Didsbury

Opened: 1931 as a cinema
Converted: 1948-50 as a theatre
Reopened: 1972 as Horniman Theatre

Opened as a cinema in the pit of the depression in 1931, the Capitol Theatre was beset by problems. Following a fire in April 1932, the theatre was reopened in August 1933. It boasted one of the most advanced cinema organs in the country. It was also fully equipped for live theatre and was used occasionally for pantomimes and amateur performances, including productions by the Didsbury Amateur Operatic and Dramatic Society.

A reversal in cinematic fortunes in 1948 temporarily brought new hope to live entertainment. In response to the "film famine", the management of the Capitol, A.B.C., scheduled the theatre to undertake live stage productions. The manager at the time, Mr. Buckle, optimistically spoke of a resurgence of stage shows, and expressed his intention to present opera and ballet following the opening performance of *Me and My Girl*. But this excursion into live theatre was not sustainable, and cinema presentations resumed after 1950.

However, in the light of changing leisure patterns, the building's future as a cinema was also uncertain, and in 1956 it was converted into a television studio. This was closed in 1968. The newly formed Manchester Polytechnic acquired the premises in 1971 for its School of Theatre. Live theatre returned to The Capitol in the more permanent form of the Horniman Theatre. This presented performances by the college's students. Productions saw the early stage appearances of Julie Walters, Bernard Hill and David Threlfall. In 1987 the theatre reverted to its former name.

CASINO

See People's Concert Hall.

CENTURY THEATRE COMPANY

See University Theatre.

CHORLTON PAVILION

Wilbraham Road, Chorlton-cum-Hardy

Opened: 1904
Renamed: c.1911 as Chorlton Theatre
and Winter Gardens

Opened as the Chorlton Pavilion in 1904 this theatre is best remembered as the Chorlton Theatre and Winter Gardens. The proprietors, Messrs Maitland and Broadhurst, offered "high-class promenade concerts, every evening at 7.45" with matinees every Wednesday and Saturday at 3.30. The admission was typically 2d and 6d.

Handbill for production at Horniman Theatre, 1983.

CHORLTON REPERTORY THEATRE CLUB

Formed: 1946
Dissolved: 1953

The Chorlton Repertory Theatre Club was established in 1946. Although the club had no theatre of its own, it offered a weekly repertory performed by a professional company. Initially it used a large room connected with the Lloyd Hotel, Chorlton. The brainchild of two actors, James Lovell and Arthur Spreckley, the club played to full houses in Chorlton. However, problems pre-empted by the sacking of Lovell began to mount, and by 1952 the club was making a loss. Membership declined. Blame was laid at the door of television and bad weather, but Alan Bendle observed that "of the 1952 performances, perhaps only six out of the fifty-two were successful". A professional producer was employed in 1953, who immediately gave the company notice. In 1954 the Chorlton Theatre Club became home to the Piccolo Theatre Company which brought to Manchester a group of young actors, designers and directors, many of whom were to leave their mark on the world of theatre. For two seasons productions that included *The Women Have Their Way* (Frank Dunlop) and *Maria Marten, or The Murder in the Red Barn* (Richard Negri) provided an early opportunity to assess the talents of individuals who were to become more familiar to Manchester audiences.

CITY THEATRE
Mount Street

Opened: 1844 as Cooke's Circus – converted to temporary Theatre Royal
Reverted to Cooke's Circus: 1845
Reopened: 1847 as City Theatre
Closed: 1850

Occupying a site in Mount Street, the City Theatre was originally known as Cooke's Circus. The wooden structure was probably built around 1842, and was used for equestrian and dramatic performances. The first proprietor, Thomas Cooke, established a circus there around 1844, the company being drawn mainly from his family. Cooke was a poor businessman, and the enterprise soon experienced financial difficulties.

In 1844, following the fire at the Theatre Royal in Fountain Street, the circus was converted into a temporary Theatre Royal which opened with *She Stoops to Conquer* in June 1844. This arrangement continued until Knowles had built his new theatre in Peter Street. The circus resumed in 1845 following the opening of the new Theatre Royal, but Cooke was soon declared bankrupt and forced to sell. The circus company continued performing, but with no greater success, and quit the theatre in the autumn of 1847. The building reopened as the City Theatre on 11th December, 1847, finally closing down in February, 1850.

See also Theatre Royal, Fountain Street.

CONTACT THEATRE
See University Theatre.

COMEDY THEATRE
See Gaiety Theatre.

COOKE'S CIRCUS
See City Theatre

EMPIRE, ARDWICK
Hyde Road, Ardwick Green

Opened: 1904, as the Ardwick Green Empire
Renamed: 1935 as the New Manchester Hippodrome
Closed: 1961

The Ardwick Green Empire music hall was opened on 18th July 1904. The proprietors were The Manchester Hippodrome and Ardwick Empire Limited, the managing director being

Programme extract showing prices and show times for the New Manchester Hippodrome, 1939.

Oswald Stoll. The first manager was Will Collins. The theatre had been built in a mere eight months by the sole contractors, Alfred Hodgkinson of Hulme. It seated around 3,000 people.

Offering a traditional range of music hall acts and pantomime, the Empire presented comedians, singers, animals, acrobats, and even water spectacles. The theatre aimed at high quality but popular entertainment. Entry to the twice-nightly performances cost sixpence for the grand circle, fourpence for a pit seat, and threepence for the Gallery. Admission prices were lower on Wednesdays, Thursdays and Fridays. The standard of accommodation seems to have been considerably better than those found in the older theatres such as the Alexandra Music Hall. The opening night began with Fred Karno's celebrated company of comedians, including Fred Kitchen and Cossie Noel, followed by the band of the First Regiment, Caucasian Guards "supported by the most powerful company ever seen at any vaudeville theatre outside London". The enjoyment of the entertainment was aided by Frank Matcham's architecture which provided good acoustics, ventilation, space and safety with an attractive decor. In terms of entertainment, a *Manchester Evening News's* correspondent described the theatre in the following terms: "The management of the Ardwick Green Empire . . . maintains a high standard of entertainment . . . none of the dozen entertainers falling below average merit, and some of them rising high above it".

Following the closure of the Hippodrome on Oxford Street, the theatre was reopened as the New Manchester Hippodrome in 1935. It was extensively modified to preserve the atmosphere of the original Hippodrome rather than the Empire itself, and was described at the time as: "The Hippodrome, renewed at the Ardwick Green in the structure of the Empire". Early performances at the New Hippodrome featured Larry Adler, Max Wall, and Joe Loss and his band. Popular musicals such as *The White Horse Inn*, *Desert Song* and *The Student Prince* also attracted large audiences.

In 1959, Moss Empires sounded a prophetic warning – a five week closure due to a "shortage of suitable shows and variety acts". On 22nd April 1961, after *Tokyo* had completed its two-week run, the theatre was closed. Responding to the ever-changing world of commercialised leisure, plans for a bowling alley were made, but a fire in February 1964 made the idea untenable. The building was demolished in the autumn of that year.

See also Manchester Hippodrome, Oxford Street.

FIRST EXCHANGE
Market Street

Built: 1729
Demolished: 1792

Before the eighteenth century the history of theatrical performances in Manchester remains obscure. Detailed evidence is the exception though references have been made, for instance, to a version of the *Robin Hood* play being performed during Queen Mary's reign. But as in other provincial towns it was only in the eighteenth century that the theatre became an established feature of a rapidly expanding community. Before the opening of purpose-built

Manchester's First Exchange, built 1729, demolished 1792.

theatres plays were performed by travelling companies from London and Dublin in the Exchange. The first Exchange, built by Sir Oswald Mosley in 1729, contained a large room suitable for such productions, and it was frequently used by itinerant performers and showmen. Dramatic performances held there included Farquhar's *Recruiting Officer* (1743) and *Macbeth* (1750). An undated fragment of a handbill for *The Fair Penitent* shows seats to have cost 1s 6d for the pit and one shilling for the gallery.

Following the opening of the Marsden Street Theatre (1753-1775) and the Theatre Royal, Spring Gardens (1775-1807) the Exchange was more used for exhibitions and musical performances. The Exchange was demolished in 1792.

FOLLY THEATRE OF VARIETIES
See Alexandra Music Hall.

FORUM THEATRE
Wythenshawe Civic Centre

Opened: 1971

Manchester Corporation began to finalize its Wythenshawe Civic Theatre project in the late 1960s, although the idea for a theatre in Wythenshawe had been put forward by David Scase in the mid 1950s when he was artistic director of the Library Theatre. Following the success of the Library Theatre, the intention of the Libraries Committee was to build a professional repertory playhouse in Wythenshawe, a district that contained some 100,000 people – almost one-sixth of the city's population. The idea was to complement the Library Theatre's "high-brow" productions with more accessible entertainment that would appeal to ordinary working people.

The new theatre cost £750,000 to build, being part of a major £1.5 million civic project. Seating almost 500, the theatre was equipped with dressing rooms, workshops and lighting and sound equipment, a distinct improvement on the Library Theatre's "rabbit runs". The Forum was officially opened on 28th July 1971, in a ceremony conducted by Lord Rhodes of Saddleworth. In addition to the theatre, the Civic Centre also housed two halls, a lending library and a swimming bath. Other facilities included a restaurant, licensed bar and coffee bar. Following the tragic death of Tony Colegate, David Scase returned as the artistic director of both Library and Forum Theatres. Projects were devised which would link the Forum with the local community, including "teach-ins" for children and teachers during productions and experimental shows. A film club was also organised by the Manchester Film Theatre, which began, appropriately with the screening of *A Funny Thing Happened on the Way to the Forum* in October 1971.

The first play to be performed was John Hale's *Lorna and Ted* on 22nd September 1971, part of a season which included Samuel Beckett's *Waiting for Godot*, David Mercer's *After Haggerty* and Ray Galton and Alan Simpson's adaption of Obaldia's *The Wind in the Sassafras*

Trees. The aim of the early seasons was to present plays with a local theme, featuring well-known actors where appropriate. First season attendances were a shade below the 50 per cent capacity anticipated, but rose as the theatre's reputation grew. Plays were presented jointly with the Library Theatre, opening alternately every three weeks. The idea of the two theatres having separate companies performing a separate programme of plays was dropped, a critic noting that to deprive Wythenshawe audiences of serious drama by staging nothing but light entertainment would have been tantamount to a "separate but equal" cultural policy. The new arrangement meant that productions would still go to both theatres, but open at the Forum. This was considered preferable to the former arrangement, where shows opened at both theatres on following nights and were then swapped over after three weeks.

It was the theatre's public profile that caused early criticism by Ken Farrington and other actors, who accused the Corporation of neglecting to publicise the Forum's productions. However, performances including Stanley Houghton's *Hindle Wakes* and Sean O'Casey's *The Shadow of a Gunman* were well received. The Forum also presented pantomimes and musicals. Productions by local theatre groups, including the Manchester Polytechnic School of Theatre and Manchester Youth Theatre, were also mounted.

Subsequent performances have included Pete Townshend's rock opera *Tommy*, European premieres of Stephen Sondheim's *Follies* and *Pacific Overtures* and Alfred Uhry's play, *Driving Miss Daisy*.

In recent years financial problems have beset the theatre, with the City Council having been forced to withdraw its annual grant. The highly successful run of Sondheim's *In the Woods* was feared to be the last major production that the Forum would be able to mount. Sondheim lent his support to the theatre during this difficult period. Sponsorship from Manchester Airport has alleviated short-term worries, and there are plans to make the theatre an indepen-dent charitable trust, presenting a mixed programme of touring theatre productions, films, concerts, Christmas shows and musicals.

See also Library Theatre.

FREE TRADE HALL
Peter Street

Opened: 1856
Hall destroyed by enemy bombing: 1940
Free Trade Hall reopened: 1951

Manchester has had three Free Trade Halls, of which the third, opened in 1856, is the most famous and abiding. This building was designed by Edward Walters in the Palladian style, typified by its deep arches, pedimented windows and tympanum of figures and Ionic columns, and it provided the rapidly expanding town with a large public hall, at a time when such a facility was badly needed. The hall was used as a venue for meetings, concerts and other entertainments. Occasionally dramatic performances were given, especially by

Handbill for a production at the Free Trade Hall featuring Charles Dickens, 1857.

amateur companies. Charles Dickens was no stranger to the stage of the Free Trade Hall. He appeared on two occasions in 1852 though his best remembered visit was in the production of Wilkie Collins's *The Frozen Deep* on 21st and 22nd August 1857. Charles Dickens managed and acted in the production, appearing as Richard Wardour in *The Frozen Deep* and in the title role of *Uncle John* in Buckstone's farce which followed the main play. Charles Calvert's farewell performance took place at the hall, Calvert appearing in *Julius Caesar* and *Much Ado About Nothing*. By the Edwardian period, novelties such as Everett's *Science and Mystery* and Harry H. Hamilton's *Excursions* made their appearance.

On 22nd December 1940, the Free Trade Hall was badly damaged by fire caused by enemy bombing. After the war the hall was rebuilt under the direction of Leonard C. Howitt, City Architect, and was reopened on 16th November 1951; Sherwood Edwards's sculptures on the rear of the building serving as a reminder of the variety of entertainments associated with the hall. Since its rebuilding, the Free Trade Hall and the Hallé Orchestra have become even more synonymous, although the hall has also been used for dramatic recitals such as Elspeth Douglas Reid's *One-Woman Theatre* and Emlyn Williams's portrayal of Charles Dickens in February 1960.

GAIETY THEATRE

Peter Street

Opened: 1878 as Gaiety Theatre of Varieties
Reopened: 1884 as the Comedy Theatre
Reopened: 1903 as the Gaiety Theatre
Closed: 1921

Although the Gaiety Theatre is renowned for its years under Miss Horniman (1908-1921), its history begins some three decades before. In 1878 the first Gaiety Theatre of Varieties was opened, under the management of Edward Garcia. Situated close to the corner of Peter Street and Mount Street it was built on the site of an earlier circus. Although offering reasonable accommodation and programmes of entertainment, the Gaiety apparently enjoyed only moderate success. What was to prove to be the first chapter of its history was brought to an end in June 1883, when the building burned to the ground.

The previous lessee, Edward Garcia, built the new Comedy Theatre on the same site. Designed by Alfred Darbyshire, the new building was built in brick, with full provision for dressing rooms and prop rooms. Great attention was paid to safety and fire precautions. It cost £15,000 and could hold some 1,500 people. The theatre opened on 22nd December 1884. Under his sole proprietorship, Garcia sought to bring high quality entertainment to the theatre. Performances by the Calvert Dramatic Society and productions featuring players such as the American actress Genevieve Ward may have helped raise the tone of the theatre, but the prices were concomitantly higher, going all the way up to two guineas for a private box. When Garcia withdrew due to financial problems, J. Pitt Hardacre became the new lessee. A policy of popular prices was introduced, and he called in the architect Frank Matcham to modernize the theatre. For a time, the theatre enjoyed a revival in its fortunes, with popular dramas and pantomimes. as the main bill of fare.

In the opening years of the century the theatre became the centre of a number of scandals centring around Pitt Hardacre. These contributed to a change in owners and name. Pitt Hardacre's farewell performance was held on 30th March 1903. The theatre, now controlled by the United Theatres Company, who already operated the Theatre Royal and the Prince's Theatre, reopened on 26th October 1903 as the Gaiety Theatre, under the management of Oscar Barrett. The first production was F. Osmond Carr's *The Rose of the Riviera*. After 1905, programmes carried the legend: the "Theatre of Cottonopolis". A successful period followed, with performances such as Seymour Hicks's *Talk of the Town* and pantomimes like *The New Aladdin*, although offstage, the theatre became embroiled in one of the great scandals of Edwardian Manchester involving the city's Chief Constable, Robert Peacock. However, the United Theatre Company, like previous owners, were unable to obtain a liquor license for the theatre and had the additional commitment to its two other Manchester theatres. The theatre was subsequently sold to Miss Horniman in 1908. The last performance prior to Miss Horniman's company taking up residence was

Interior of Comedy Theatre, Peter Street, 1900.

a benefit for the manager, H. M. Thorburn, on 6th April 1908.

Under the guidance of her young manager, Ben Iden Payne, a Manchester man, Miss Horniman became the founder of England's first permanent repertory theatre. Initially her Playgoers' Theatre Company had performed in the Midland Hotel Theatre, but it was at the Gaiety, re-designed by Frank Matcham, that their reputation was secured. The theatre reopened on 7th September 1908. Early performances, beginning with *When the Devil was Ill*, were received with enthusiasm – as was Miss Horniman herself. The "actors' nursery" included among others: Lewis Casson, Sybil Thorndike, Herbert Lomas, Milton Rosmer, Irene Rooke, Basil Dean and Charles Bibby. The *Manchester Evening News* amusingly honoured her as No. 78 of their series "Men of Mark", reporting her intention to "make money out of the Gaiety Theatre, not lose it". Miss Horniman's desire "to discover an English dramatist" would prove to be the necessary impetus for the encouragement of a 'school' of playwrights which included Stanley Houghton, Harold Brighouse, Allan Monkhouse, Judge Edward Parry, H. M. Richardson and Basil Dean. Houghton's *Hindle Wakes* (1912) was an outstanding success, as was Frank Rose's *The Whispering Well* (1913). The work of John Galsworthy was also regularly performed. Favourable reviews and word of mouth gradually broadened the audience to include more than simply those "intellectuals from the University, vegetarians, nature-lovers, weekend hikers in the Derbyshire hills and general marchers in the advanced guard of public opinion" who were said to have been prominent among the theatre's early supporters.

Miss Horniman's activities in Manchester have been admirably charted by Rex Pogson and, more recently, Sheila Gooddie. Her eccentricity is nowhere better demonstrated than in her personal emblem, an ornate six pointed star – an astrological symbol representing "Glory, Fame and Success". However, success was more elusive than fame and glory, and by the time of the First World War the Gaiety was experiencing problems. After 1917, Miss Horniman leased the Gaiety to other companies, maintaining a semblance of control by vetting scripts. Plans to revive her company at the Gaiety never came to fruition, and in 1920, Miss Horniman's seemingly inexhaustible purse was shown to have a bottom. She sold the theatre for £52,500 to Abe Hollander, owner of the Futurist Picture House. The "Glorious Failure" had yielded to the future. The final performances of May 1921 consisted of a season of Stanley Houghton plays. The curtain came down leaving Cottonopolites and others to pick over the bones of this remarkable theatrical adventure. Not all were willing to puff the Horniman years as a success.

James Agate, who had begun his career as a theatre critic writing for the *Manchester Guardian*, blamed The Gaiety for "letting Manchester down", puncturing the idea that there ever was a Manchester school of drama:

Houghton's Hindle Wakes was a bright flash in what turned out to be a very small pan, and Harold Brighouse never followed up Hobson's Choice. The only first-class work . . . was Allan Monkhouse's Mary Broome.

The Gaiety Picture House opened on 18th July 1921. Live performances – a short season of pantomime followed by some variety and music hall entertainments – were tried in the late 1930s but the theatre soon reverted back to a cinema. Presentations included a 54-week run of *Gone With the Wind*. Harry Buxton sold the property in 1959, and it was demolished in August of that year. The new building, Television House, represented the future world of entertainment though the inclusion of two plaques reminded visitors of the site's connection to an earlier period of the entertainment history of the city.

The last picture show at the Gaiety, Peter Street, June 1959.

Gentlemen's Concert Hall, Peter Street, 1897, shortly before demolition.

GENTLEMEN'S CONCERT HALL

Lower Mosley Street

Opened: 1830
Closed: 1898

The existence of exclusive Gentlemen's concerts has been traced back to amateur musicians who met in a tavern in Market Street around 1770, moving to the Amateur Concert Room in Fountain Street in 1777. Support for the concerts was such that by the early nineteenth century the public concerts were recognised as an important social occasion at which "the numerous assemblage of fair 'Lancashire witches' listening to the 'Concord of sweet sounds' from the parterre and the gallery, afford a rich treat to the eyes of admirers of female beauty, while the lovers of harmony are gratified by the excellence of both amateur and professional performers". Increased support made it possible to consider erecting a new building. A substantial and impressive new building in Lower Mosley Street, designed in the neoclassical style by Richard Lane, was opened on 30th August 1830. It was paid for by the society's subscribers. The concerts allowed Manchester to assess the talents of Liszt, Paganini and Chopin, and they were one of the key factors in determining Charles Hallé to settle in the town. In addition to musical performances, occasionally recitations of plays, sometimes in costume, were given. But the hall's chief significance in the theatrical history of the city lies in the fact that it was the venue for the first performance in Manchester by the small but influential Independent Theatre Society on 24th February 1893, allowing local audiences the opportunity to experience and assess the work of Ibsen and others.

The hall was sold to the Midland Railway Company in 1897 for £22,600 on the understanding that a new concert hall would be incorporated into the new hotel that the company proposed to build on the site. The final musical concert in the hall was held in March, 1908.

See also Midland Hotel Theatre.

GRAND JUNCTION THEATRE

See Hulme Hippodromes.

GRAND PAVILION
and PALACE OF VARIETIES

Peter Street

Opened: 1883
Closed: 1916

Also known as the Grand Pavilion and Theatre of Varieties, this theatre was opened in November, 1883 by Edward Garcia. Early documentary evidence suggests that Garcia was unable to make it pay and for a time it operated as a circus. Garcia eventually went bankrupt. After 1893, under the management of E. H. Jones, the theatre began to expand its repertoire into variety acts in addition to traditional circus acts, for example, the Paddock Troupe of Lady Trick Cyclists. Seats were typically 1s 6d for boxes and reserved seats, one shilling for the lounge, 6d for the upper circle and 3d-4d for the pit. Other curiosity acts of this period included Percy Walsh, Champion Circle Walker; John Lloyd, "the original Singing Collier"; Mechanical Mannikins, "The Living Pigmies"; Lensorama Dramatic Recitals; Serpentello, "Marvellous Contortionist" and Professor Alberto, "Premier Wizard".

Although Jones introduced dramatic sketches and operatic overtures into these programmes, the emphasis was on variety featuring acrobatics, comedy, dance, ventriloquism and even shooting exhibitions. But the Grand continued to struggle particularly as new theatres and variety halls opened

Interior of the Grand Theatre, Peter Street, 1900.

in the city-centre. It closed for a period in 1905-6. The rise of the kinema was to prove irresistible and in March 1916 the Grand closed as a theatre and was re-opened as a cinema. It continued to operate as a cinema into the 1920s when the building was demolished to make way for a church.

GREEN ROOM THEATRE
Whitworth Street West

Founded: 1926
Re-established: 1983

The Green Room Society was founded in 1926 to foster interest in drama and allied arts, to encourage new writers, and to present plays of quality, including the "classics". Basil Dean and Sybil Thorndike were instrumental in the society's formation. Initial interest waned after a few years and the society was maintained by the enthusiasm and commitment of Anderson Kennedy, Vera Woods and Winifred Michaelis. However, despite its many setbacks, the society was to continue until 1982.

Initially the society had no theatre of its own, performing in various halls around the city. Its first permanent theatre was situated in Liverpool Road, and it was there that the society established a reputation for challenging productions. This success was short-lived as the war dispersed the membership and saw the theatre destroyed by enemy bombing. After the war, the society established the Green Room Theatre in a Cheapside cellar. When this building was demolished in 1961, new premises were found, this time in the form of an old schoolhouse on Little Peter Street, Knott Mill. Yet another setback occurred in 1964 when the theatre was damaged by fire, but it was quickly repaired and reopened. In the 1970s the active membership continued to decline and the society was finally dissolved in 1982.

In 1983, the theatrical promoter Jeremy Shine began to redevelop the Green Room with the aim of maintaining the experimental traditions of the original society. Shine's company, Radiator, set about providing Manchester with its only fringe theatre. The concept was expanded to embrace the idea of a full performing arts centre. After several years of performing as the Green Room, giving 200 shows in 20 different venues around the city, the company moved into the new Green Room on Whitworth Street West. The new venue was a former railway viaduct. The conversion, undertaken by the architects Fletcher Priest, produced a 170-seater auditorium with retractable tiered seating, a bar, cafe and studio facilities for classes and workshops. The initial cost was £278,000.

The first performance took place on 6th June 1987 with a production of *Skat*. Since then the Green Room has become a leading north-west venue for alternative theatre and experimental arts, presenting plays, cabaret, modern dance, reviews, comedy and music shows. Companies to have performed at the theatre include DV8 Physical Theatre, North West Dance Umbrella, Raw Cotton Theatre Company, El-Hakawati (a Palestinian company), Vox Theatre

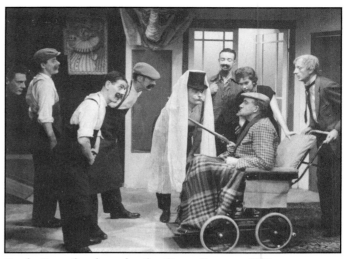

Production of a farce by the Green Room, c.1953.

Company, Soyikwa Theatre Institute (South African), Lip Service and Gay Sweatshop.

HARTE'S THEATRE
Grey Mare Lane, Bradford

Opened: 1894
Closed: 1899

Harte's Theatre or Grand Theatre and Fairyland was built around 1894. It is likely that this wooden structure was originally a circus, which the lessee Charles Harte, converted into a music hall and theatre. The opening performance took place on August 3rd, 1896, and featured the Musical Palmers, Silveno, "The Man with the Mysterious Finger" and the comedian, Will Atkins. A place on one of the form seats cost 2d, 4d or 6d. The theatre burned down on 7th January 1899.

HIPPODROME
Oxford Street

See Manchester Hippodrome.

HORNIMAN THEATRE
See Capitol Theatre.

HULME HIPPODROME
Warwick Street, Hulme

Opened: 1902 as the Hippodrome
Renamed: 1905 as the Grand Junction Theatre
Renamed: 1929 as the Junction Picture Theatre
Renamed: 1951 as The Playhouse
Renamed: 1956 as the BBC Playhouse Theatre
Closed: 1986
Reopened: 1991 as the Nia Centre

Situated in Hulme, the Hippodrome and the Grand Junction, as they were initially called, formed the core of W. H. Broadhead's theatrical empire. Both buildings were erected between 1900-1901, and were connected by an arcade which was flanked by the Broadhead company's offices.

The theatre on Warwick Street was opened on 6th October 1902 as the Hippodrome. Early performances concentrated on variety acts whilst the Grand Junction Theatre in Preston Street staged dramatic productions. Whilst the patrons at the Grand Junction were enthralled by dramas such as *The Grip of Iron*, the Hippodrome audiences were amused by acts such as the Seddons, "Grotesque Jugglers", Maud Dewey "Champion Whistler and Mimic", and George Macintosh "Champion Clog Dancer of the World".

Prices of admission at Warwick Street were typically: one shilling for the orchestra stalls, 6d for the circle and 2d for the gallery. This arrangement of performances between the two theatres continued until 1905, when the names (and entertainments) were, rather confusingly, interchanged. Thereafter the theatre began a new career as the Grand Junction Theatre presenting drama as the theatre in Preston Street had formerly done.

Advertisements in the *Manchester Programme* indicate that the building ceased to be used as a theatre around April 1929. It was then opened as the Junction Picture Theatre.

In 1950, both theatres were purchased by the James Brennan Circuit and were extensively renovated and redecorated throughout. The Hippodrome in Preston Street continued with variety shows, and the theatre in Warwick Street was renamed The Playhouse and once again became a live theatre.

Frank H. Fortescue, described as "one of the few men who have ever been able to make repertory pay" was invited by the Brennan Circuit to bring one of his seven companies to the Playhouse. Ironically, it was Brennan who had forced Fortescue out of the adjacent Hippodrome in Preston Street when he bought both theatres. The first performance, given on 22nd January 1951, was *The Happiest Days of Your Life* (the popular, and only recently filmed, farce) featuring Franklyn Scott and Neena Harvey.

The Playhouse was bought by the BBC in 1956 for the production of radio and television shows. The first television production in January 1956 was a revue entitled *Call It A Day*. In 1970 the BBC added a Wurlitzer organ transferred from the Empress Ballroom, Blackpool. Over the years, stars associated with the BBC Playhouse included the Beverley Sisters, Les Dawson, The Grumbleweeds, Tom Mennard, Cardew Robinson, Bill Waddington and Harry Worth. The last performance at the Playhouse was *A Farewell to the Playhouse* broadcast on 25th August 1986.

The building's connection with entertainment did not end with the closure of the Playhouse, as plans were announced to use it as a home for the Nia group.

See also Broadhead Theatre Circuit, Nia Centre.

HULME HIPPODROME
Preston Street, Hulme

Opened: 1901 as the Grand Junction Theatre and Floral Hall
Renamed: 1905 as Hulme Hippodrome
Renamed: 1942 also known as 2nd Manchester Repertory Theatre
Reopened: 1950

Broadhead's theatre on Preston Street was opened as the Grand Junction Theatre on 7th October 1901. Complementing the light entertainments given in the adjacent Hippodrome in Warwick Street, the Grand Junction's dramatic presentations formed a dual centre to the Broadhead Theatre Circuit. Early performances included *A Fatal Crown*, *On the Frontier* (adapted from James Fenimore Cooper's novel *Last of the Mohicans*) and *Uncle Tom's Cabin*. The theatre also staged opera, pantomime and occasional variety shows. In 1905 the two theatres exchanged identities, the Grand Junction becoming the Hippodrome and Floral Hall. The theatre then concentrated on variety shows with bioscope, recitations and music hall "revivals".

Over the years, the theatre has had its share of controversy. In 1939, a performance of *Man About the House* given by the Holmfirth Amateur Players was criticised for being staged on Good Friday. Its gritty themes of unemployment, domestic conflict and the means test – performed by mill workers – were considered unsuitable by the Chief Constable of Manchester. Between 1942 and 1949 the theatre was also known as the Manchester Repertory Theatre. Performances by Frank H. Fortescue's players predominated during these years, including Ivor Novello's *Fresh Fields*, Walter Greenwood's *Love On The Dole*, Harold Brighouse's *Hobson's Choice* and George Bernard Shaw's *Candida*.

In 1950, the theatre was purchased by the James Brennan Circuit. It was renovated, decorated and entirely re-carpeted.

Hulme Hippodrome (later the Junction Theatre), 1960.

The gallery was reopened and the installation of tip-up seats increased the capacity to nearly 2,000. The Floral Hall was also refurbished. Fortescue left the theatre, which once again concentrated on variety. The Hippodrome reopened with a production on Monday 20th February 1950 which included Billy Reid and Dorothy Squires. Although variety and pantomime topped the bill at the Hippodrome, Fortescue's company once again returned after 1956 following the sale of The Playhouse to the BBC.

Controversy once again surrounded the theatre following its sale to Bill Benny, "a cigar-smoking, former all-in wrestler" who converted the theatre into a "revue bar" (or less euphemistically, strip club) in 1960. This short, colourful period was dogged by disagreements with musicians and the authorities, who promptly banned his "pioneering" production of *Striperella*, "a striptease pantomime". Benny sold the theatre to the Mecca chain for around £50,000 in 1962. The theatre was then used as a bingo hall and casino, with occasional variety and amateur performances being given.

INTIMATE THEATRE

See Library Theatre.

JUNCTION THEATRE

See Hulme Hippodrome, Warwick Street.

KING'S THEATRE

Stockport Road, Longsight

Opened: 1905

Closed as theatre, later became cinema: 1933

The King's Theatre, also known as the King's Opera House, was the last Broadhead Theatre to be built in Manchester. It opened in October 1905. Early performances

King's Theatre, Longsight, c.1910.

featured Ernest Montefiore and his company (Montefiore had been acting manager at the Comedy Theatre) performing a "musical and dramatic scena" entitled *The Little Colonel*, a piece set in the Boer War.

As with the other Broadhead theatres, the emphasis was upon variety, but the theatre also staged opera, circus and "straight" dramatic performances. The King's also ran local talent competitions. Local favourites appearing at the theatre include Harry J. Clifford and Marie Paxton of the Broadhead Repertory Players, and music hall stars such as Hylda Baker, Billy Danvers, Sid Field, Jimmy James and Fred Karno's Company. Dramatic performances included *No, No Nanette* and Frank H. Fortescue's production of *The Gypsy Vagabond*.

In 1932 the theatre was sold to H. D. Moorhouse and became part of his circuit of cinemas and theatres. The King's was reopened on 1st August 1932 under the management of George Barrasford, the former manager of the Piccadilly Cinema. Despite Moorhouse's intention to bring "the best in the world of variety, revue and dramatic plays", live performances continued for less than a year. The last live performances at the King's were Lena Brown's "Crazy Week" (May 8 1933) after which the theatre was closed. The cinema remained in business for 31 years, eventually closing in 1964.

The building was later used by the Ardri Irish Club (1965-6), but following a fire in September 1966 it lay empty and was eventually demolished in the autumn of 1973.

LESLIE'S PAVILION

Dickenson Road, Rusholme

Opened: 1904

For over thirty years "Leslie's" was a landmark of Rusholme. Owned and operated by Harry Leslie, a former cotton worker from Cornholme, whose talents as a ventriloquist persuaded him to leave the relative security of the mill for the more precarious world of showbusiness. But it was his organisational rather than his performance skills that eventually established his reputation. In 1904 he started his concert parties in Rusholme, aiming to bring a dash of seaside entertainment into the drab world of the working-class suburbs. Initially, the performances were given in a marquee but their success soon led to a more permanent building in the grounds of the Rusholme Hotel.

A wide range of entertainers were permed by Leslie to provide what proved to be a popular entertainment. Regular performers who appeared at the Pavilion included Leslie Henson, Mariott Edgar and Milton Hayes. Although tastes in entertainment were changing, Leslie's concert-party format continued into the 1930s bearing out the opinion he expressed to a local newspaper reporter that "not everybody cared for super-modernity". In 1936 the Pavilion's 32nd birthday was celebrated with a broadcast by the BBC. The Pavilion eventually closed in the early years of the Second World War.

Programme for Tilly of Bloomsbury, Leslie's Pavilion, Rusholme.

LIBRARY THEATRE

Central Library, St. Peter's Square

Opened: 1947

Although the immediate history of the Library Theatre may be said to begin in the years after the Second World War when the lecture theatre built into the basement of Manchester Central Library was converted into a theatre, its deeper origins lie the debates that had taken place earlier in the century, in Manchester and other cities, about the necessity and legitimacy of spending rate payers' money on a municipal theatre. When the Central Library was opened in 1934, a large lecture hall had been provided alongside other facilities in order to ensure that it would serve as an important centre of cultural activities for the citizens of Manchester. The unique location and size of the lecture theatre, which seats 300, made it an ideal small venue for future performances. During the Second World War the theatre was used as a studio by the BBC and was restricted to day engagements such as the Ministry of

Information lunch-time commentaries.

After the war, the Manchester Corporation Act of 1946 empowered the Libraries Committee to fully utilise the theatre for "lectures, exhibitions, concerts, displays, and the performance of stage plays for or in connection with the advancement of art, education, drama, science, music or literature". For theatregoers, who were finding serious drama more difficult to find in a city-centre increasingly dominated by the cinema and the variety theatres, this was was seen as the first step towards the establishment of a professional civic theatre. The *City of Manchester Plan* had already recognised the importance of such a cultural facility. After considerable discussion it was decided that the theatre would be let at a nominal charge to a non-profit making repertory company. The theatre was opened under the director André van Gyseghem, who managed the Manchester Intimate Theatre Group. The first performance, *The Seagull*, took place on 11th February 1947. Not every-body welcomed the appearance of a new theatre in the city-centre and among the objectors were the Theatrical Managers' Association concerned about the impact on existing theatres. Walter Payne, Chairman of the Theatres National Committee, emphasised the present vulnerability of local theatres by observing that "fog in Manchester might be sufficient to put a theatre on the wrong side, financially". The theatre's opponents feared that it would be offering unfair competition because of its subsidies and "privileged status" as part of Manchester Corporation, and they argued that productions should be restricted to amateur societies. Various companies subsequently occupied the Library Theatre in association with the Arts Council, but mounting losses eventually led to a withdrawal of support.

In August 1952, the Libraries Committee took the bold step of taking direct control of the theatre through their officer, the City Librarian. The first performance under the auspices of the Libraries Committee was Oscar Wilde's *The Importance of Being Earnest* in November, 1952. Much of the theatre's early success was due to the talent and drive of David Scase, and for a number of years up to the early 1960s it attracted near capacity audiences and was able to declare a book-keeping profit. Even so, the theatre still found it necessary to justify its role in the cultural life of the city. As David Colley, the City Librarian argued:

Should we then let live theatre die in the provinces? . . . Should we confine our local entertainments to the brisk trade in vulgarity of twice-nightly revues, farces and nude shows to fill for tired businessmen and women the gaps which inevitably occur on radio and T.V.? I think not. Manchester men and women will ensure that this one theatre will live and eventually blossom into the civic theatre which a few people for a long time have dreamed of.

In more recent years the challenge has been how to survive in a world where central government has re-defined the status and financial position of local authorities. But the city council has not lacked courage, notably in establishing a second theatre in Wythenshawe. Despite repeated financial cutbacks and restrictions both the Library Theatre

Production of Billy Liar at the Library Theatre, 1962 starring Patrick Stewart, Donald Gee and Diane Collett.

and the Forum Theatre have continued to produce plays in line with the overall philosophy of entertaining and educating local theatregoers.

See also Forum Theatre.

LONDON GRAND MUSIC HALL

See Queen's Theatre, Bridge Street.

MANCHESTER HIPPODROME

Oxford Street

Opened: 1904

Closed: 1935, later site of Gaumont cinema

The Hippodrome, Manchester's "three-in-one" theatre, was opened on Boxing Day, 1904. The first performance included comedy and musical acts, a canine entertainment, and making full use of the theatre's facilities, an equestrian sketch, *Tally-Ho! A Hunting Sensation in Four Scenes.* Designed by Frank Matcham, the theatre was capable of staging music hall, circus or water spectaculars. The building cost £45,000 and held 3,000 people in comfort. It occupied a site between Great Bridgewater Street and Chepstow Street, the "front door of Manchester" opening onto Oxford Street, a site previously associated with Hengler's Grand Cirque. "Matchless Matcham's" design was a *tour de force* of theatrical architecture. The principal entrance was through a front colonnade, approached by marble steps. Walls, staircases and balustrades were also in marble. The architecture throughout was in the Arabesque style. The auditorium itself was 60 feet wide, expanding to 100 feet at the gallery. A sliding panel in the roof over 30 feet long was used to ventilate the theatre. The design featured chorus galleries which could be occupied by choristers when productions required it. The stage was 42 feet in diameter covered by a four-ton mat. Beneath the stage was a circular tank capable of holding 70,000 gallons, heated by its own furnace. The tank was raised by a hydraulic ram. Also hidden from the audience beneath the auditorium was stabling for one hundred horses, and a lions' den.

Under the control of the quietly spoken impresario, Oswald Stoll, the Hippodrome became one of the principal homes of variety in Manchester, presenting comedy, concerts, tragedy, opera-bouffe, ballet, musical comedy,

Hippodrome, Oxford Street, shortly before its conversion into the Gaumont cinema, 1934.

pantomime, vaudeville, circus, puppet shows and water spectaculars as well as more conventional dramatic performances. The early years of the theatre were largely devoted to variety, circus and water spectaculars. The unchallenged king of the water shows was Albert Hengler, who performed spectacles such as *The Redskins* and *Mexico*. Famous performers who have appeared at the theatre include Sarah Bernhardt, Ellen Terry, Charles Manners, Lily Langtry, Pavlova, Phyllis Dare, Gracie Fields, George Robey, Mark Hambourg. George Formby was to find early success at the Hippodrome, and was so fond of the theatre that a reproduction of the proscenium was placed over his grave!

In 1933, the theatre produced a season of Shakespeare's plays, under the management of A. S. Whittaker and producer Stanley Bell. The production of *Julius Caesar* featured Valentine Dyall as Octavius, Godfrey Tearle as Marcus Antonius and Basil Gill as Marcus Brutus. *The Merchant of Venice* featured Franklin Dyall as Shylock and Marie Ney as Portia. Whittaker acknowledged that tastes in popular entertainment were changing, and after an abortive attempt to "make the Hippodrome one of the best variety theatres in Britain", the theatre was closed down. It was demolished in 1935 to make way for the Gaumont cinema. However the Hippodrome did not die as it was recreated in the Ardwick Green Empire, which thereafter became known as the New Hippodrome.

See also Empire, Ardwick.

MANCHESTER REPERTORY THEATRE

See Rusholme Theatre.

2nd MANCHESTER REPERTORY THEATRE

See Hulme Hippodrome.

MANCHESTER YOUTH THEATRE

See University Theatre.

MARSDEN STREET THEATRE

Marsden Street

Opened: 1753
Closed: 1775

Although the first Theatre Royal may be regarded as the official acceptance of a theatre in Manchester, the Marsden Street Theatre deserves its title "Manchester's first theatre". It appears that the theatre was opened in 1753 on the corner of (what was to become) Marsden Street and Brown Street. One account asserts that Richard Elrington brought his company to the theatre in that year, but the success of the company and the theatre were to be short-lived. Aulay Macaulay had apparently "obtained a license with difficulty from the not best-tempered magistrate". Elrington and his wife came up with the idea of issuing bills advert-ising the opening of the theatre on 3rd December 1753 "with a play and other amusements for the benefit of the Infirmary". This proved to be a considerable error of judgement. The authorities were outraged at Elrington's implication that the recently-established hospital required the charity of "rogues and vagabonds", and ordered the company to leave Manchester within twenty-four hours.

The theatre appears to have remained virtually unused until February 1758 when there was a performance of *Acis and Galatea*. In the following year James Whitley, who was to have a considerable impact on the development of theatre in the Midlands and the north of England brought his itinerant company to Manchester without offending the authorities. However, these early years were not without trouble including in April 1760 when a man was killed in a duel arising from an argument at a rehearsal!

Between 1762 and 1764, Ross and his London company performed at the theatre staging the then popular Shakespearean productions such as *Romeo and Juliet,* and *King Lear* with Colley Cibber's happy ending. Whitley returned to the theatre in 1766, and in the following years he helped to establish its reputation. The first Manchester production of *She Stoops to Conquer* was given in the 1773-4 season. Other authors favoured by Whitley included Fielding, Garrick, Farquhar and Foote. Whitley also encouraged local writers.

The theatre itself was basic, and seats cost two shillings for the pit and one shilling for the gallery. As in other towns he visited, Whitley was instrumental in introducing more modern theatrical practices. The stage was kept clear during performances, and patrons were not allowed backstage. Heating was also installed because, as an early extant programme explained, "complaints have been made as to the coldness of the Pit, there will be Stoves for the future, to render it warm". He also introduced private boxes priced at three shillings, for which, it was suggested patrons purchased "the privilege of being burned or crushed to death in fires, panics, or riots, since they could never open the box when such disasters occurred".

Whitley's most successful seasons ironically preceded the granting of the Royal Patent to the first Theatre Royal in Spring Gardens. Elizabeth Farren's performances raised the quality of productions to new heights. Whitley fought against the imminent competition of the new theatre, offering a subscription which effectively cut prices by half, with the addition of wax illumination and new curtained boxes. This did not reverse the decline, and the final performance at the theatre was on 12th May 1775. Whitley left Manchester and continued as a successful provincial producer until his death in 1781. Farren and her sisters together with other Marsden Street players moved to the new Theatre Royal.

The theatre was converted to a newsroom and tavern, and later served as that most quintessential of Manchester buildings, a cotton warehouse. The building was demolished in 1869.

METROPOLE THEATRE

Ashton Old Road, Openshaw

Opened: 1898
Closed: 1938

The Metropole Theatre was W. H. Broadhead's second Manchester theatre. It was opened on 6th April 1898, Thursday of Passion Week. The first play to be performed was *A Woman's Victory*, "a drama of the Veldt". "The Met" was originally designed to accommodate 2,000, but this was later reduced following the installation of 'tip-up' seats. The original configuration was of a gallery with plain wooden form seats and a pit with covered 'running' seating. Prices were similar to those of the Osborne Theatre, and at the time of opening ranged from 3d. in the Gallery to £1.10s for a private box. Advertisements emphasised that the building was "heated and lit with electricity".

Entertainment included drama, opera, variety, comedy and pantomime. Artists who appeared at the theatre included

Interior of the Midland Theatre.

Martin Conway, Nicodemus and John Lawson. F. S. Gilbert and his Grand English Opera Company also performed at the theatre. Plays included *The Face at the Window* and *A Royal Divorce*. Later presentations featured Walter Greenwood's *Love On The Dole* which was advertised as "the greatest human play of the century" and starred Wendy Hiller as Sally Hardcastle.

In its heyday, the "Met" drew in capacity audiences, following the successful Broadhead balance of popular drama and variety. The final series of performances was given by the Fortescue Players in the summer of 1938. The last performance was B. F. Rayner's *The Dumb Man of Manchester*, after which the Metropole closed as a theatre.

The building was sold to H. D. Moorhouse on 22nd August 1938, to form part of his cinema circuit. During the theatre's conversion to a cinema, 12 lorry loads of backcloths, scenery and props were distributed to other theatres. The cinema remained in business for another 21 years, before closing on 14th April 1959, a time when Moorhouse was shutting down many other cinemas. The building was demolished in 1962.

MIDLAND HOTEL THEATRE

Peter Street

Opened: 1903
Closed: c.1920

When Charles Heywood sold the Gentlemen's Concert Hall to the Midland Railway Company, it was on the understanding that "a new, more commodious, and more convenient hall would take the place of the old one". The new theatre reflected the lavish standards to be found in the rest of the Midland Hotel. Performances at the theatre – it seated some 1,000 people in comfort – began shortly after the hotel opened in September 1903.

Undoubtedly the most important contribution to the city's theatrical heritage was the series of performances given by Ben Iden Payne's Playgoers' Theatre Company. This would prove to be the foundation of the new repertory theatre company based at Miss Horniman's Gaiety Theatre. The programme for the company's opening performance begins with a statement of Payne's aim of "drawing back to regular theatre-going all those who have lost this habit". Much of Payne's philosophy would shape Miss Horniman's thinking, especially the intention to establish a wide-ranging permanent repertory theatre with an emphasis on good acting, intelligent and careful productions and popular prices. The first performance of the company at the Midland was Charles McEvoy's *David Ballard* with Iden Payne in the title role. The company went on to present plays including: Basil Hood's *The Great Silence* featuring Basil Dean; A. R. Williams' *The Street*, "a symbol of man's degradation"; and George Bernard Shaw's first play, *Widowers' Houses* featuring Lewis Casson and Charles Bibby. The critics were generally enthusiastic in their reception of Payne's company, describing *David Ballard* as "a brilliant comedy, brilliantly played". Equally well received was a series of Irish plays by the Irish National Theatre Society, directed by W. B. Yeats. This series strengthened what might be termed the theatre's "Horniman connection" given her well known links with the Irish Dramatic Movement in general, and W. B. Yeats in particular. Productions included Synge's tragedy *Riders to the Sea*, Lady Gregory's *The Gaol Gate* and Yeats's *The Hour Glass*. This represented a distinctive contribution to the Edwardian theatre and is too easily viewed as a prelude to the Gaiety experiment.

But the Midland also mounted less taxing entertainment including regular appearances by H. G. Pelissier's "Follies", often performing burlesques at which the tongue-in-cheek warning was given: "an egg-proof curtain will be lowered at least once during the performance for the protection of the artistes". Other companies appearing included the German Comedy Company, the Ryder Boys Old English Comedy Company, the Victorian Amateur Players, the Lewis Waller Amateur Dramatic Club and the Manchester Ship Canal (Staff) Operatic and Dramatic Society. Later shows included Ashton and Mitchell's "Kinemacolor" film of *Imperial India*. Such presentations were to pave the way for a cinema project which saw the end of live entertainment at the theatre by 1920. It was later used as a cinema and a ballroom.

See also Gentlemen's Concert Hall, Gaiety Theatre.

MINOR THEATRE
See Theatre Royal, Spring Gardens.

NEW AMPHITHEATRE
See Theatre Royal, Spring Gardens.

NEW MANCHESTER HIPPODROME
See Empire, Ardwick.

NEW PAVILION
See Theatre Royal, Spring Gardens.

NEW QUEEN'S THEATRE
See Opera House.

NEW THEATRE
See Opera House.

NIA CENTRE
Chichester Road, Hulme

Opened: 1991

The Nia Centre developed out of the initiatives begun by Moss Side residents in the 1970s to promote and celebrate Afro-Caribbean culture. When the BBC vacated the

Playhouse in 1987 the opportunity arose of acquiring a permanent building. The Playhouse was purchased in 1988 and work on converting the building began in the following year. Supported by the City Council, Arts Council and the Hulme and Moss Side Task Forces the building was transformed into an impressive arts centre – including a 900 seat theatre – a significant addition to the city's cultural facilities. It opened on 22nd April 1991. The architects were Mills' Beaumont Leavey, and their transformation of the old theatre was recognised by a Community Enterprise Scheme Architectural Award from the Royal Institute of British Architects in November 1992. Under the direction of Morenga Bambata the Centre has developed a broad and innovative programme of black theatre, dance, concerts and films. Although the Centre has not been immune from the social problems of the area, it provides a cultural experience that contrasts with the tabloid perspectives of Moss Side and Hulme. Nia is Ki-Swahili for "purpose".

OLYMPIA
See Royal Osborne Theatre.

OLYMPIC THEATRE
Stevenson Square

Opened: 1838
Closed: 1841

Also known as the Royal Olympic, this theatre opened on Boxing Day 1838. The original site was occupied by a wooden structure erected by the Cooke family. Thomas Cooke later mounted another venture in Mount Street (see City Theatre). Later the building became The Tabernacle, in which Dr. Samuel Warren, having been expelled by the Wesleyan Conference, founded the Wesleyan Methodist Association. The "Warrenites" eventually moved to a chapel in Lever Street.

In 1838 a brick building was erected on the site, and it was here that the Olympic Theatre was opened. Its short life has been invariably described as a poorly judged

Drawing of the Olympic Theatre, Stevenson Square, c.1840.

and ill-fated venture. The theatre comprised an unattractive pit and gallery in which good quality entertainment was the exception rather than the rule. However, popular performers occasionally lit the artistic gloom including G. V. Brooke, a fine Shakespearean actor of the day. Possibly more to local tastes were T. "Jim Crow" Rice, a singer and dancer, James Carter "the Lion King", and Andrew Ducrow. Other performers included Cony and Blanchard, melodramatic actors, and the ever-popular George Preston, who later appeared on the boards of the Queen's Theatre in Spring Gardens.

The theatre was also used for various amateur performances, which were described as "lively". Cotton workers were among the groups to stage amateur performances. The audiences, presumably drawn from the surrounding working-class neighbourhoods, had a sharp sense of good entertainment, and were usually quick to participate in the performance by heckling, booing and pelting the unfortunates on the stage with fruit and assorted refuse.

The bad luck that dogged the theatre later struck one of its main attractions. In 1841, James Carter was seriously injured by one of his lions during a performance. The ensuing pandemonium culminated in a mass stampede out of the theatre. The theatre closed in the same year and was purchased by Robert, William and Frederick Faulkner, who opened a drapery business there.

OPERA HOUSE

Quay Street

Opened: 1912 as The New Theatre
Renamed: 1915 The New Queen's Theatre
Renamed: 1917 The New Queen's and Opera House
Renamed: 1920 The Opera House
Closed: 1979
Reopened: 1984

The plan to provide Manchester with "a new Shakespearean Theatre and Grand Opera House" was made public in 1911. London and Manchester businessmen were behind the "New Manchester Theatre Ltd." which dangled profits of £9,000 before the public to raise the £40,000 it was estimated would be needed to build the city's largest theatre. Theatrical expertise came locally in the form of Richard Flanagan, and nationally in the person of the actor-manager, Lewis Waller, both renowned for their revivals of Shakespeare. The building of the theatre in Quay Street was completed rapidly in spite of the labour troubles of 1912. The architects were H. Farquharson, and Richardson and Gill who were said to have been influenced by the work of Charles Cockerill, architect of Manchester's Bank of England. The theatre could hold some 3,000 people. The audience sought by the New Theatre was indicated in seat prices ranging from sixpence in the gallery to five shillings in the stalls. *Kismet* opened the theatre on Boxing Day, 1912; a lavish production that was much enjoyed even though the theatre's much publicised state-of-the-art machinery was experiencing teething problems.

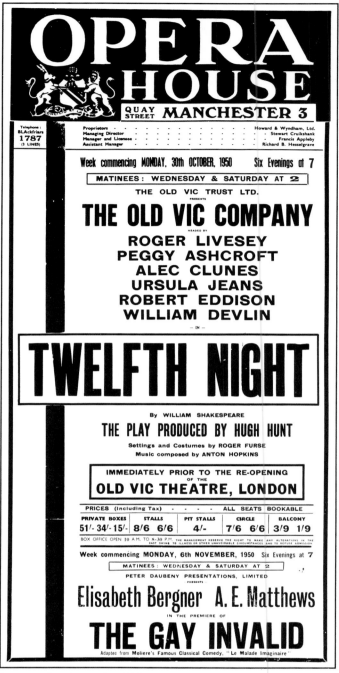

Poster advertising the Old Vic Company at the Opera House, 1950. The producer was Hugh Hunt.

The New Theatre had hardly time to establish its presence in the city before war broke out. During the war it underwent a number of changes of name and ownership. In 1915 it was purchased by the United Theatres Company and it was renamed the New Queen's Theatre. Films now began to be offered as well as live entertainment. The former included epics such as D. W. Griffith's *Intolerance* and more patriotic fare such as *The Kaiser, The Beast of Berlin*, advertised as "a tremendous photo-drama that strips naked the soul of history's maddest murder king". But these years were best remembered for the visits of an equally combative individual, Thomas Beecham. The highlight of the spring months became the visits of Beecham's

Opera Company whilst his autumn promenade concerts also drew large audiences.

The theatre was renamed The Opera House in August 1920, opening with the *Rose of Araby*. It experienced mixed fortunes in the 1920s and underwent a change of ownership when Howard & Wyndham took it over in 1931. Money was invested to improve facilities but these were difficult times and during the early 1930s the theatre closed for the summer months. Its fortunes recovered by the end of the decade not least because of the improving strength of the regional economy. There were also strong productions. In 1938 it could boast a hatful of world premières including Noel Coward in *Operette*; Emlyn Williams and Sybil Thorndike in *The Corn is Green*, and Leslie Banks in *Goodbye, Mr. Chips*.

During the 1940s and 1950s the Opera House was firmly established at the centre of Manchester's theatre world. Its programme remained varied though it enjoyed particular success with its staging of new American musicals including *Oklahoma* (1947), *The King and I* (1956) and *West Side Story* (1958). (*South Pacific*, which played to packed houses twice in the 1950s, brought to Manchester an unknown actor, Sean Connery, who might have forsaken the world of the theatre and be remembered for a different number had he taken up Matt Busby's offer to play football at Old Trafford.) Alongside musicals the theatre hosted regular visits from the Sadlers Wells and D'Oyle Carte companies. Memorable plays included Orson Welles and Peter Finch in *Othello* and John Gielgud as Lear. However not all productions impressed, and in the case of the Salford-teenager Shelagh Delaney a visit to the theatre led her to think that she could do better: the result was *A Taste of Honey*.

The 1960s proved a dismal decade as audiences declined, some lost to television, others to subsidised theatre, and the costs of installing high-class London shows escalated. The theatre closed for a number of weeks during its jubilee years of 1962, including some outside the notoriously difficult summer months. It was an ominous trend that even the success of shows like *My Fair Lady* could not conceal. By 1966 Howard & Wyndham were looking at schemes to redevelop this and other increasingly valuable city-centre theatre sites (including the Royal Court, Liverpool) that they owned. Discussions with Manchester City Council over the possibility of a subsidy came to nothing, especially as the City was looking to establish a new regional arts and opera centre. The "image" of the Opera House did not suit the mood of the times; a theatre moreover that "no longer commanded a prominent place in "Theatre Street" and was quite inadequate as a home for a permanent ballet company". In a move that clearly disturbed the sensibilities of a section of the city's theatregoing public, Howard & Wyndham applied for, and eventually received, a bingo license for the problematic summer months. This "shrine of culture" needed a level of investment that neither private nor public sources seemed willing to provide. Even an energetic Friends organisation whilst drawing attention to the importance of the theatre could not disguise the need for new money. Basic amenities required attention: "the notorious

Macbeth starring John Gielgud at the Opera House, 1942.

Circle loo flushing clobbers any concentration one may have had at the outset", as one regular patron remarked.

The 1970s proved a disastrous decade, as the theatre appeared to jump from crisis to crisis. The debate about whether Manchester could support both the Opera House and the Palace Theatre became even more intense. Rumours about the fate of the two theatres proliferated. For a time in 1977 it appeared that the essential support of both the Arts Council and the Greater Manchester Council would lead to the closure of the Palace rather than the Opera House. However, after convoluted and difficult discussions involving public bodies and the decisive intervention of Raymond Slater, Chairman of Norwest Holst, it was decided, to the surprise of many, to support the Palace. The Opera House would not receive either private or public money to continue operating. Howard & Wyndham took the decision to sell the theatre to Mecca who intended to use it as one of their bingo social clubs. What many thought was to be the last theatrical performance at the Opera House took place in April 1979.

But the transformation of the theatre into a bingo hall was to be a short one. Early in 1984 it was announced that the Palace Theatre, boosted by its phenomenal success, had decided to buy the Opera House and reopen it as a theatre specifically to stage long runs of musicals. The refurbishment work required was modest compared to what had been required at the Palace, and the Opera House began the second volume of its history as a theatre with a production of *Barnum* in October, 1984. This proved to be the first of a number of record-breaking musical shows that might amongst other things cause future historians to examine managerial practises and styles of the theatre's different owners.

45

OSBORNE THEATRE

See Royal Osborne Theatre.

PALACE THEATRE

Oxford Street

Opened: 1891
Reopened: 1913
Closed: 1978
Reopened: 1981

Almost from the time the plan was announced of building a Manchester Palace of Varieties in January, 1889 there was opposition. The promoters' intention was to provide Manchester audiences with the experience of the modern music hall. A site on the corner of Oxford Street and Hunt Street (later Whitworth Street) was acquired for the new theatre. Opposition to the scheme came from local temperance groups, led by the Methodists. The letter columns of the local press overflowed with expressions of concern that the music hall, rather than being an innocent form of recreation, threatened public morality, a place where drink would be available and young men might find themselves in the company of fast women. Other critics played on the fact that the scheme for the Palace of Varieties was being driven by metropolitan businessmen. It was a well organised lobby and congratulations were soon being sent to local magistrates on their "manly stand against an insidious attempt by London speculators to impose upon the community a fascinating and dangerous incentive to drunkenness".

In spite of this local opposition, the theatre was eventually opened in Whit Week, 1891, with a somewhat restrained programme of 'grand ballet'. Seat prices starting at sixpence in the upper circle indicated that the promoters were looking towards the working classes to fill its seats. Whilst opposition to the Palace did not subside, and it was repeatedly refused a drinks licence, the carefully directed protests of the moral minority appears not to have stopped the masses coming to enjoy what others described as "good, clean wholesome vaudeville entertainment". Among the stars who performed were Little Tich, Vesta Tilley, Fred

Interior of the Palace of Varieties, 1900.

Kitchen, Dan Leno, Marie Lloyd and George Formby Senior though those with keen eyes and sharp memories would also recall that Charlie Chaplin appeared at the Palace in 1903. During the Edwardian years new music halls appeared in Manchester, including most notably the New Theatre in 1912 (See Opera House). It was partly in response to this competition that the theatre was entirely rebuilt in 1913. Bertie Crewe, one of the country's best-known theatre architects, was in charge of the rebuilding, producing an auditorium in what was identified as "the French-Neo-Grec Style". Whatever its architectural pedigree the auditorium oozed luxury and the modern. Electric lighting showed off the fittings and confidence was such that there was no anxiety about even installing a biograph chamber.

After the First World War there was a gradual but persistent shift away from music hall entertainment towards the presentation of more conventional drama. During the 1940s and 1950s the Palace became *the* Manchester venue for a number of touring companies. By the late 1950s the theatre was experiencing financial difficulties as the tastes and addresses of audiences changed, production costs rose, and there was increasing difficulty in securing those star names that would ensure a well-filled auditorium. The theatre relied even more on the profits from touring companies, including opera and ballet, and, of course, the Christmas pantomime. During the 1960s the theatre continued to decline and rumours of takeover and the closure of the theatre appeared with greater frequency. It was a situation that was being repeated in many provincial towns though in Manchester the debate was increasingly seen in terms of whether it would be either the Palace or the Opera House that would survive to present live theatre and shows in the city centre. The "Battle of the Two Theatres" was a fierce one with a public agenda that did not always match the private lobbying and discussions that went on with central and local government bodies. It was difficult to predict the outcome, though by 1977 it appeared to many observers that it would be the Opera House that would survive. However, in a surprise move, following the intervention of the local businessman, Raymond Slater, it was the Palace that was to survive. Slater purchased the

theatre and handed it over to a trust. Plans to carry out an extensive refurbishment, both in the auditorium and backstage, were put in motion. Bob Scott, whose administrative skills had been amply demonstrated at the 69 Theatre Company and then the Royal Exchange Company, was brought in as managing director to oversee the changes. The Palace re-opened on 18th March 1981. It pursued a policy of attracting high quality touring companies with star names. This was combined with a professional marketing strategy that widened the geographical and social catchment areas from which its predecessor had drawn its audience. It proved an immediate success, box-office records were repeatedly broken and after only a few years plans were put in motion to reopen its old rival, the Opera House.

PEOPLE'S CONCERT HALL

Lower Mosley Street

Opened: c. 1846
Closed: 1897

The People's Concert Hall stood on the site now occupied by what Mancunians will always call the Midland Hotel. It was one of Manchester's most popular music halls offering the varied programme of vocalists, comedians and dancers that made up a typical evening's entertainment at the Victorian music hall. It began life as the Casino and was known as "The Old Cass" and also, after its proprietor T. B. Burton, as "Burton's Night School", apparently because it attracted the young who ought to have been studying at a neighbouring evening school. It was a substantial building, capable of holding some 3,000 people. Admission charges ranged from 2d in the pit to 6d in the lower gallery and boxes. One visitor recalled that when crowded "the dense, solid vapour which takes place of the ordinary air is something indescribable." Contemporary accounts suggest a lively audience, whose eagerness to participate in the performance, at one time compelled the management to protect the orchestra with wire netting, a defence against objects thrown at the stage. The hall closed in 1897 when the Midland Railway Company purchased the site to erect the Midland Hotel.

The People's Concert Hall, Lower Mosley Street.

PLAYHOUSE

See Hulme Hippodromes.

PRINCE'S THEATRE

Oxford Street

Opened: 1864
Closed: 1940

As suited a city where profit and free trade were pursued energetically, the Prince's Theatre was founded by businessmen looking to make money by opening a new theatre, broadening competition in a theatrical world dominated by the Theatre Royal and the Queen's. The risks involved in such a project were considerably reduced by obtaining the services of Manchester's most celebrated actor-manager,

Prince's Theatre, Oxford Street, 1936.

Charles Calvert. Initial capital of almost £20,000 saw the speedy construction of the Prince's on a commanding site close to the corner of Peter Street and Lower Mosley Street. Edward Salomons was employed as the architect. Calvert soon fulfilled his promise to provide "dramatic entertainment of the highest class". The doors opened on 15th October 1864. The first production of *The Tempest* with its lavish scenery, costumes, music (part of the score featured the work of the young Arthur Sullivan) and bowdlerized text did not disappoint. Calvert's Shakespearean productions became synonymous with the Prince's. Popular success resulted in strong profits: in 1869 the interior of the theatre was extensively reconstructed – including the addition of 300 seats in the upper circle – under the supervision of Alfred Darbyshire. A frieze over the proscenium painted by H. Stacy Marks depicting Shakespeare flanked by muses and his principal characters was the highlight of the new interior.

The ownership of the theatre changed hands on a number of occasions and for a time it operated in conjunction with other local theatres. George Harris Browne, a wealthy

Demolition of Prince's Theatre.

American who lived in Manchester, was a key figure in these financial dealings. The theatre was eventually sold to its rival, the Theatre Royal Company for £42,500 though this also proved to be a short alliance as in 1892 the New Prince's Theatre Company Ltd. bought the theatre back. The twenty years before the First World War represented a remarkable period in the theatre's history. The Prince's developed a reputation for staging extraordinary pantomimes: in 1890-1 *Babes in the Wood* did much to accelerate the career of "Little Tich". Robert Courtneidge's appointment as manager in 1896 ensured that this standard would be at least maintained, and the Princes's pantomimes remained a high point in the city's cultural calendar. Courtneidge also revived Shakespeare. In the 1901 production of *A Midsummer Night's Dream* his eight-year-old daughter, Cicely, playing Peaseblossom, began a stage career that was to continue for the next seventy years. The Edwardian period was to see further success when the musical comedies of the Irish-born theatre manager, George Edwardes, arrived from Daly's Theatre: the Guv'nor's productions proving as popular in Manchester as they had been in London.

The Prince's laid claim to two theatrical innovations: firstly, the introduction of 'tip-up' seats, and, secondly, the practice of 'early doors' whereby patrons could by purchasing a more expensive ticket enter the theatre early, thus avoiding the discomfort of the crush (and the Manchester weather) outside.

The post-war years were less successful as the theatre fought to attract audiences in an increasingly competitive leisure market. By the 1930s the Prince's was clearly struggling to meet the challenges of newer entertainment, most obviously represented by the lengthening queues outside the city-centre's super-cinemas. At the end of 1935 the United Theatre Company sold the Prince's to Shaftesbury Developments Ltd. for £50,000. The theatre was leased to John Buckley, a local cinema owner, who tried to provide a different type of production by bringing in the Manchester Repertory Company. This arrangement did not last long. Buckley soon left, nursing substantial losses, convinced that Manchester did not want legitimate theatre. But even the more-experienced hands of Prince Littler, one of the country's leading impresarios, who took over the management in 1937, could not find the theatrical and financial formula that would make the theatre viable. Falling audiences and rising costs eventually led to the curtain coming down for the final time in April 1940. The "Moloch of Cinema" appeared to devour another victim when it was announced that the Prince's was to be sold to the ABC cinema company. The theatre was demolished but the plan to erect a super-cinema on the site was interrupted by German bombers and wartime restrictions. After the war the idea of building a cinema was abandoned, and following years of dereliction it was the concrete mass of Peter House that rose on the corner of Peter Street and Lower Mosley Street.

PYBUS MUSIC HALL

See Harte's Theatre.

QUEEN'S PARK HIPPODROME

Turkey Lane, Harpurhey

Opened: 1904
Closed: 1952

Built on the site of an old tramshed, the Queen's Park Hippodrome was opened on 25th April 1904. The Hippodrome presented variety, drama, pantomime and revue. Dramatic performances included Walter Greenwood's *Love On The Dole*, George Bernard Shaw's *Pygmalion* and *Mrs. Warren's Profession*.

In later years, drama gave way to revue and eventually the "sizzlingly saucy" French variety of Barry Piddock. Like many of the smaller suburban theatres, the Queen's Park Hippodrome fell victim to the cinema and in 1952 the theatre closed. For many years this sad, crumbling ruin lay empty, causing much local consternation as it fell prey to constant vandalism. The building was finally demolished in January 1966.

1st QUEEN'S THEATRE

See Theatre Royal, Spring Gardens.

QUEEN'S THEATRE

Bridge Street

Opened: 1870
Closed: 1890
Reopened: 1891
Closed: 1911

The Queen's Theatre occupied a site that had long connections with popular entertainment. Hayward's Hotel had stood on the site and in the early Victorian period had became known for its musical and other entertainments. In December 1862 the hotel was converted into the London Music Hall. The music hall operated for a few years until it was taken over by Edward Garcia who converted it into the Royal Amphitheatre and Circus. But Garcia's efforts to present profitable entertainment were unsuccessful. In June 1870 the building was demolished, and a new theatre – the Queen's – built. The new theatre was designed by Edward Salomons, who was to develop a considerable reputation as a theatre architect in the north west. Its interior, suitably ornate with scroll plasterwork and crimson satin much in evidence, accommodated some 1,400.

Initially the theatre was operated by Frederick Barney

Queen's Theatre, Bridge Street, 1903.

49

Egan and Walter Rainham who sought to match productions, seat prices and audiences. A popular feature was its regular Shrove Tuesday production of *George Barnwell*, a Georgian moral tale that apparently only brought out the devil in Victorian audiences, especially the students of Owens College. One memorable performance came with the visit of Mapleson's Royal Italian Opera Company though for one theatregoer the overriding memory of the Queen's was its "pungent-musty aroma which under no circumstances could be mistaken for Eastern perfume". Frequent changes in management pointed up the struggle to develop a large and loyal audience.

In August 1890 the building was severely damaged by fire – fortunately not during a performance. The theatre was rebuilt and under the control of Pitt Hardacre it opened in the following spring on 28th March. Shortly afterwards it was leased to Richard Flanagan who ran the theatre until its closure in 1911. Flanagan, no doubt influenced in part by Charles Calvert for whom he had worked at the Prince's, took the risk of reviving Shakespeare. In 1896, *Henry IV* (Part I) was the first revival with Louis Calvert as Falstaff. After a hesitant start these revivals caught the imagination of "cultured Manchester", and even attracted talent scouts from London. Flanagan's productions were renowned for their sumptuous costumes, colourful scenery and dramatic music, but given their high production costs and the theatre's "moderate" seat prices they courted financial crisis. On one occasion Flanagan settled a debt by paying

Frederick Smith in costumes, a transaction that inadvertently led to the establishment of what became one of the city's best-known firms of theatrical costumiers.

Apart from the early winter programme of Shakespeare, Flanagan offered a range of other productions searching to capture an audience. On occasions, even plays with a local theme were tried. In May 1904, for example, *Old Manchester, or When James I was King* was staged, a play based on Harrison Ainsworth's novel *Guy Fawkes*. Whether this romantic historical drama dealing with the love of Humphrey Chetham for Viviana, daughter of Sir William Radcliffe, attracted and found approval among the city's antiquarians is not made clear in the reviews. As the theatre's lease came to an end, Flanagan's energies were channelled into other enterprises including a scheme to build a new Queen's on Bridgewater Street. The final performance at the Queen's was *Hamlet* on 24th June 1911.

RENOLD THEATRE

Sackville Street

Opened: 1962

This theatre is situated in the Renold Building of the University of Manchester Institute of Science and Technology (UMIST). It was opened in 1962, part of the development of the college's modern campus. The building was designed to house a number of lecture theatres, including a 500-seat theatre which could be used for dramatic performances. It was chiefly used by student groups and amateur societies. In 1973 the Manchester Drama Group, which had worked at The Stables until its unexpected closure, put on a production of *Joey Love*. Although in recent years it has served the university as a large lecture theatre it is still occasionally used by various drama groups.

ROYAL CASINO

See People's Concert Hall.

ROYAL EXCHANGE THEATRE

St. Ann's Square

Opened: 1976

The immediate origins of the Royal Exchange Theatre lay in the establishment of the 69 Theatre Company in 1968 and the season of plays they produced at the University Theatre. The group, who included Michael Elliott, Casper Wrede, Braham Murray and Richard Pilbrow had come to Manchester to present new plays and, as Michael Elliott explained, to escape "from those pressures that constantly cripple ones work in London". The company's productions featuring star names – Tom Courtenay, Vanessa Redgrave, Mia Farrow – proved an enormous critical success. However the company walked a financial tightrope, and whilst it was unable to entirely cut itself off from West End audiences, their conviction to develop a permanent theatre in Manchester

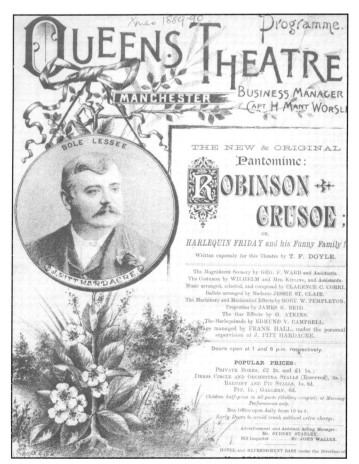

Pantomime programme, Queen's Theatre, 1889-90.

50

strengthened. Even given the overflowing talents of the group, establishing a new theatre was a considerable undertaking. Gradually the problems were overcome through a mixture of "faith and sweat", helped at crucial moments by the financial assistance of private supporters. Among the figures who played a key role in converting the idea of a new theatre into reality were Peter Henriques, a Manchester stockbroker, and Bob Scott, who served as the group's administrator from the time of its arrival in Manchester.

The group certainly did not lack vision and the imaginative decision not to *build* from scratch a new theatre but audaciously to site it in the huge cavernous trading hall of the Royal Exchange produced one of the most distinctive pieces of modern theatre architecture. The technical problems of fixing a heavy steel-framed cocoon were considerable but, as with the financial hurdles that had to be negotiated, they were overcome. Richard Negri played a key role in the design of the theatre. Levitt Bernstein Associates were the architects. The public response to the idea of theatre in the round in a novel auditorium was also growing. This relationship became more enthusiastic in 1973, when, as part of the Manchester Festival, the 69 Theatre Company moved temporarily into the Royal Exchange to perform in a (cotton) tent theatre. Work on constructing the theatre eventually started in April, 1975. It was officially opened by Lord Olivier on 15th September 1976. Since that time, the Royal Exchange Theatre Company, as it was renamed, led by a team of exceptional directors – the theatre's strength has rested on the fact that it is a directors' company – have provided an enviable list of productions characterised by originality and adventurousness, that remained close to the ideals of the founders. The achievement was all the more impressive as it occurred against the background of a sluggish economy and a parsimonious government that looked towards reducing support for the arts. If to some people the Royal Exchange represented the "unofficial National Theatre of the North", there were others who, echoing the confidence of an earlier generation who had stood in "the largest room in the world", asserted that such metropolitan comparisons were redundant.

ROYAL MINOR THEATRE
See Theatre Royal, Spring Gardens.

ROYAL NORTHERN COLLEGE OF MUSIC OPERA THEATRE
Oxford Road

Opened: 1973

The Royal Northern College of Music was created out of a merger of the Royal Manchester College of Music and the Northern School of Music. The new institution eventually occupied its purpose-built premises, part of the huge higher education campus that was rapidly developing along the Oxford Road. The building included an opera theatre and a concert hall. The first production was Gordon Crosse's *Purgatory*, based on W. B. Yeats's work, given on 20th February 1973. In addition to its musical programmes the theatre soon established a reputation as a venue for touring companies including the Royal Shakespeare Company. From its opening, dance has been one of the highlights of its varied programmes and over the last twenty years regular performances by Ballet Rambert, London Contemporary Dance Theatre and Northern Ballet Theatre have given Manchester audiences the opportunities to enjoy or puzzle over the frequently challenging repertoire of modern dance. In recent years, operatic performances mounted by the students have become increasingly popular and successful.

ROYAL OLYMPIC THEATRE
See Olympic Theatre.

ROYAL OSBORNE THEATRE
Oldham Road

Opened: 1896

Closed: 1935

The Royal Osborne Theatre was William Henry Broadhead's first Manchester theatre. Situated on Oldham Road, the opening performance was given on Easter Monday, 13th April 1896. The first play performed was *The Priest Hunter* by Hubert O'Grady. Another popular feature was pantomime, beginning with *Dick Whittington* in the Christmas season of 1896-7.

Variety and music hall shows featured acts such as Reg Harris's "The Ten Loonies Co." and "Boot Villa, featuring Widow Foot and her Five Toes". Percy Broadhead's Royal Osborne Theatre Dramatic Company performed a series of revivals which included *The Manxman* by Hall Caine, *The Lights of London* by George Sims, and Walter Howard's *Two Little Drummer Boys*.

Osborne Theatre interior, showing exit from the gallery, 1900.

Entrance to St. James's Theatre, Oxford Street, 1906.

The theatre continued successfully for many years, finally closing on 25th March 1935. The building burned down on 19th October 1958.

RUSHOLME PAVILION

See Leslie's Pavilion.

RUSHOLME THEATRE

Wilmslow Road

Opened: 1923

Closed: 1940

The early history of this theatre which was to take up the repertory banner dropped by the Gaiety is unclear. The building was originally a tramshed operated by the Manchester Tramways Company. Some time after they gave up using horses it became the Manchester Riding School. But by the late Edwardian period it appears to have been converted into a theatre (Royal Electrical Theatre) with variety acts and silent films. In 1923 Arthur Belt became manager of the theatre, which was losing audiences and in need of investment. He took what might have been viewed as the risky, almost ludicrous, decision to establish a theatre. By the end of the year the Rusholme Repertory Theatre was in business. Its first production on 26th November 1923 was Thomas Robertson's well-known 'cup-and-saucer drama' *Caste*. Gradually the facilities for both audiences and actors were improved. Maintaining a continuous programme of appealing drama was the central problem and while plays such as *Hobson's Choice* could be relied upon to boost occupancy rates, other productions left alarming gaps in the 800-seat auditorium. The gravest financial crisis came in 1933. Closure was a real possibility, not just a threat to encourage more advance bookings. Guided by Vernon Walker, the theatre was reorganised and renewed its search for diverting and entertaining plays conscious of the need to avoid "the heavy stuff". In 1935 the Repertory Company moved to the more spacious city-centre premises of the Prince's Theatre but this was not a successful arrangement and the company soon returned to Rusholme. Norman Partriege, Audrey Cameron, Charles Sewell and Wendy Hiller were among the actors and actresses associated with the theatre. The theatre eventually closed in the early months of the Second World War with the company transferring to the comparative safety of Rhyl.

ST. JAMES'S THEATRE

Oxford Street

Opened: 1884

Closed: 1907

Occupying a prominent site in Oxford Street, the St. James's Theatre and Opera House opened its doors to the Manchester public on 2nd June 1884. The first production was given by the Royal English Opera Company. The theatre was owned by James Reilly, a furniture maker, who had already recognised the profits that could be made in the new world of commercialised leisure by taking over Pomona Gardens. The opening performance was given by the Royal English Opera Company. Contemporary accounts suggest that the theatre was not well designed and various lessees appear to have struggled to develop an entertainment programme that would match the house full signs of the opening night. Edward Garcia took over the management of the theatre, and in 1886 he experimented with a programme that sandwiched a play between variety entertainments in an attempt to make the theatre a profitable venture. The ubiquitous Richard Flanagan operated the theatre from 1894 to 1905 with mixed success. In 1904 Flanagan obtained a full theatre license for the St. James's, and in December of that year he reopened the theatre with Florence West (Mrs Lewis Waller) in *Zaza*. But even these new theatrical productions failed to attract sufficiently large audiences and in September 1907, live entertainment ceased. Under the control of Sidney Price, the owner of St. James's Hall, it became one of the first Manchester theatres to be converted into a cinema.

STABLES THEATRE

Grape Street

Opened: 1969

Closed: 1971

Housed in a building that had been the stables of the historically important Liverpool Road railway terminus, The Stables was home to the Manchester Drama Group, one of the city's most innovative theatrical groups in the late 1960s. Led by Gordon McDougal, the group persuaded Granada TV to support the idea of an experimental theatre company that would work on productions, partly with a view to turning them into television plays. The Stables was a small theatre, accommodating about one hundred people. McDougal was the artistic director and his team of actors included Maureen Lipman, Richard Wilson and other artists whose faces if not names were becoming familiar to the viewers of ITV serials and plays.

The first play performed was Carey Harrison's *In A Cottage Hospital*. Productions were generally well reviewed but this path-breaking theatrical project did not put down deep roots. In 1970 Granada reviewed its policy towards experimental theatre and television, and decided to end its financial support. The theatre closed in the Spring of 1971. Various attempts, largely by student drama groups, to resuscitate live theatre in The Stables have not succeeded in seriously challenging its use as a social club for Granada employees.

THEATRE ROYAL

Spring Gardens

Opened: 1775 as the (first) Theatre Royal

Theatre burned to the ground: 1789

Reopened: 1790

Closed: 1807 as Theatre Royal

Opened: 1809 as New Amphitheatre (Bradbury's)

Opened: 1815 as Minor Theatre

Opened: 1825 as New Pavilion

Opened: 1827 as Royal Minor Theatre

Opened: 1831 as Queen's Theatre

Closed: 1869.

THEATRE ROYAL: 1775-1807

Situated on the corner of Spring Gardens and York Street, the opening of Manchester's first Theatre Royal in June 1775 stands as a milestone in the city's theatrical history. Dramatic performances had been connected with

Theatre Royal playbill, 1780; including a performance of the pantomime, The Lancashire Witches.

temporary structures, the first Exchange, and more importantly, the Marsden Street Theatre (1753-1775). The growth of popular entertainment reflected the profound social changes which were beginning to take effect as the result of industrialization, and the new patterns of urban consumption.

The Manchester Playhouse Bill, passed in May 1775, generated a fervent debate over the evils and benefits of entertainment on the populace. The Bishop of London opposed the Act, condemning playhouses as destructive to the welfare of manufacturing towns. Others saw the theatre as an antidote to religious excesses. Manchester had become a seat of Methodism, and the Earl of Carlisle argued that there was no better way than the establishment of a theatre

to eradicate that dark, odious, and ridiculous enthusiasm as by giving the people cheerful, rational amusements, which may operate against their methodistical melancholy.

The theatre opened in Whit Week, 1775 under the management of George Mattocks and Joseph Younger. The money for the building was raised from forty subscribers contributing £50 each. They managed the theatre for several years, but then followed a period of instability with the theatre being managed by a "succession of adventurers". Short periods of management by Messrs Austin and Whitlock (1781), then Miller, were followed by the return of Mattocks and Younger. After Younger's death in 1784, Mattocks passed control of the theatre to Messrs Connor and Sydney. Sydney relinquished his position in 1788 and was replaced by John Banks. Connor withdrew in 1790 and was replaced by Thomas Ward, who was to remain joint manager of the theatre until its closure in 1807. Banks retired from management in 1800, and Thomas Bellamy took his place. Bellamy appears to have been unpopular with many Manchester theatregoers "owing to an uncommon irritability of temper", and was replaced by Charles Mayne Young.

The theatre was burned down just after midnight on 19th June 1789, causing £3,000 worth of damage. Fortunately the lessee, Joseph Harrop, had the building insured. The theatre was rebuilt on the same site and reopened on 15th February 1790. Aston's *Manchester Guide* of 1804 dismissed the theatre as

a plain brick building, scarcely worthy of the populous and flourishing town to which it belongs. It is only 102 feet long and 48 feet broad, and on the appearance of a favourite performer is found most uncomfortably small for the audience.

This problem was to prove instrumental in the theatre's loss of the Royal Favours. Seats cost three shillings for a box, two shillings for the pit and one shilling for the gallery.

Whatever the building's shortcomings, it remained Manchester's main place of entertainment for over thirty years. Opening with *Othello*, the theatre boasted many famous names. Stars of the early years included Joseph Shepherd

Poster for the Minor Theatre, Spring Gardens. ➤

Minor Theatre, Spring Gardens,

Boxes 2s 6d—Upper Boxes 2s—Pit 1s 6d—Gallery 6d

This present FRIDAY, July 30,

Will be presented, for the Last Time,
An entire New Ballet Dance, written & produced by Mr. HOLLAND, called

RUSTIC COURTSHIP:

OR,

HODGE & TOMMY TITMOUSE!

Hodge - - - -	Mr. USHER
Old Hodge - - - -	Mr. CORDOZO
Tommy Titmouse - - -	Mr. HOLLAND
Old Clump - - -	Mr. HUGGINS
William - - - -	Mr. WEST
Henry - - - -	Mr. HARE
Young Robin - - -	Miss L. PINCOTT
Mrs. Clump - - - -	Mrs. HUGGINS
The Honourable Mrs. Titmouse - -	Mr. BONSALL
Fanny - - - - -	Miss PINCOTT
Jenny - - - - -	Miss COE
Little Fury - - -	Miss USHER

Villagers, &c. &c.

After which, Mr. BICKERTON will recite

BUCKS, HAVE AT YE ALL!

To which will be added, for the Last Time, the interesting Melo Drama, called the

Snow Storm;

Or, LOWINA OF TOBOLSKI.

The Govenor of Siberia - - -	Mr. GALES
Count Romanoff, Unjustly confined in the Mine of Nortschink Alexis	Mr. HUGGINS
Baron Astroff - - - -	Mr. SMITH
Yermitz - - - -	Mr. BONSALL
Ivanoff - - - -	Mr. HARE
Politviz - - - -	Mr. CORDOZO
Peteroff - (Keeper of the Dog Sledge) -	Mr. HOLLAND
Strumwald . (the Ferry Man) -	Mr. THOMAS
Michael - (an Old Attendant on Lowina) -	Mr. EVANS
Brant (Landlord of the Flask Inn) -	Mr. BICKERTON
The part of Lowina by Mrs. USHER	
Her Infant Son - - -	Miss M. USHER
Laudalin - - - -	Mrs. HUGGINS

Russian Soldiers and Peasants, &c. &c. &c.

The whole to conclude with, for the Last Time, the much admired Harlequinade, called

Harlequin's Honeymoon;

Or, LOVE, HOPE, & CHARITY.

Lubin, afterwards Harlequin - -	Mr. HARE
Indolence, afterwards Pantaloon - -	Mr. HUGGINS
Poverty - - - -	Mr HOLLAND
Lawyer - - - -	Mr. GEORGE
Margery - - - -	Mr. THOMAS
Cupid - - - -	Miss USHER
Hope - - - -	Miss L PINCOTT
Charity - - - -	Mrs. HUGGINS
Rosella, afterwards Columbine - -	Miss PINCOTT
Clown - - - -	Mr. USHER

Who, in the course of the Pantomime, will introduce his

STUD of REAL TOM CATS!

Soldiers, Sailors, Coblers, and Taylors, by the rest of the Company
Days of Performing, MONDAY, WEDNESDAY, and FRIDAY.

54

Munden, George Frederick Cooke, Mrs Jordan and Wright Bowden. Early performances of note included Mrs (Sarah) Siddons's debut as Mrs Montague in *A Word to the Wise*, Elizabeth Inchbald as *Jane Shore* and John Philip Kemble's debut as *Othello*.

Later stars at the theatre included Charles Mayne Young and Master (William Henry West) Betty – also known as Young Roscius – the young actor who caused a sensation with his remarkable performances in 1804. The Manchester audiences' discontent after Betty's departure spilled over into active hostility towards the management, particularly Bellamy. When Ward asked the public what they wanted he was told "a better company for Manchester!". The departure of the unpopular Bellamy and the appearance of first rate stars such as John Bannister, John Emery, Elizabeth and Stephen Kemble reversed the decline only temporarily. Young was a creative performer, but as manager, his introduction of novelty acts was not to all tastes.

The last performance as the Theatre Royal was given on 12th June 1807, but the planned grand finale ended in a mixture of farce and tragedy. The town's old favourite Frederick Cooke, had been engaged for six nights beginning on 15th June but noted for his drunkenness and increasingly unreliable behaviour Cooke spent his advance without ever appearing.

The first Theatre Royal lost the Royal Favours which were granted to the new theatre in Fountain Street. Subsequent incarnations always languished in the shadow of the new Theatre Royal that had the sole right of producing dramatic plays in the town.

NEW AMPHITHEATRE: 1809-1812

The theatre was reopened as the New Amphitheatre or Bradbury's Amphitheatre on 11th September 1809. The new proprietor, Robert Bradbury was a celebrated clown of his day, and was the first of several managers to take up the challenge of the limitations imposed on minor theatres by the Royal Patent.

The theatre itself, despite renovation in 1801, was simply too small, and the site provided no room for extension. The expanding prosperity and sheer numbers of a new urban workforce in Manchester meant larger audiences – demands the theatre could not meet. Bradbury knew that he could not emulate the range and quality of productions found at the Theatre Royal in Fountain Street. His productions were unashamedly populist, featuring variety acts and pantomime. Seats cost four shillings for a box, three shillings for an upper box, two shillings for the pit, and one shilling for the gallery. Acts included acrobats, equestrian feats, bird imitations, harlequin (often featuring Bradbury himself) and serio-comic musicals. Notable amongst early performances were pieces such as *The British Patriot, or, The Jubilee of 1809*, which was accompanied by naval and military processions. This patriotic offering was reinforced in the same programme, where Bradbury boasted of "a superb hall decorated with our most splendid victories, and a most brilliant transparency of our beloved sovereign". Such displays of loyalty were part of the debate

Theatre Royal playbill for a charity performance of The Merchant of Venice in aid of the British army, 1793.

between loyalists and radicals in these unstable years. As one of the most public of places, theatres were often the arena within which such disagreements were fought.

Despite the production of weekly pantomimes and extra-theatrical activities such as the riding lessons given by Walford the theatre was forced to close.

MINOR THEATRE: 1815-1825

The theatre was acquired by Mr. Roe who restored the building to a condition similar to its Theatre Royal days. It re-opened as the Minor Theatre on 3rd July 1815. Typical prices were: boxes three shillings, upper boxes 2s 6d, pit two shillings and gallery one shilling. Entertainments ranged from melodramas such as *Marmion* based on the poetry of Walter Scott, to novelty entertainers including Monsieur and Madame Godeau who performed on the tight rope, Carter, "the eminent pugilist" offering demonstrations of "the noble science of sparring", and Bannister and Cooke with their equestrian troupe. Other presentations included R. E. Lloyd's astronomy lectures illustrated by the "Dioastrodoxon" to "the dulcet tones of the celestina". Less edifying performances included Mon-sieur Alexandre, who performed "a scene from the dentist in which he will imitate the groans of the patient"! The Minor Theatre reopened as the New Pavilion in June 1825.

NEW PAVILION: 1825-1827

The first performance at the New Pavilion took place on 27th June 1825. Although the theatre had been redecorated, the "entire change of entertainments" offered by the new manager, Montagu Corri, remained entirely familiar. Ballet (featuring the Corris themselves), melodrama, pantomime, comic song and dance, pyrotechnic displays amongst other things dominated the programmes.

ROYAL MINOR THEATRE: 1827-1831

The New Pavilion was reopened as the Royal Minor Theatre on 18th June 1827. Under the management of John Neville, drama was given more emphasis. Although performances of *Macbeth* were interspersed with song and dance, choruses and extended scenes of combat, it is clear that the theatre began to challenge the limitations of minor theatre status imposed by the Royal Patent.

Richard III (performed 6th November, 1827) was suitably "altered and adapted" by Neville "to the limits of a Minor Theatre" – a conscious decision to produce genuine drama. This was clearly a period of transition that would be continued in the form of the Queen's Theatre.

QUEEN'S THEATRE: 1831-1869

The Queen's Theatre was opened on the 30th May, 1831, initially under the management of William Beverley. After Victoria ascended to the throne in 1837, the laws relating to the Royal Patent were relaxed, allowing minor theatres to produce dramatic stage plays. This change of fortune was marred by what Swindells called "one of the few tragedies of real life associated with the stage in Manchester" when Mr Campbell who was appearing in the drama *Lilian*, was accidentally shot and killed by a property man.

The 1840s saw a period of relative success under the management of John Sloane. Much of this revival was due to the fact that the Theatre Royal in Fountain Street had been burned down in May 1844. Early players at the Queen's Theatre included the Beverleys, Mrs M'Gibbon and Edmund Kean. The eminent actor John Vandenhoff was another favourite. Helen Faucit also made her Manchester debut at the Queen's in 1845. Another popular performer was Miss Fife, who returned to the Queen's following the destruction of the Theatre Royal.

The audience's traditional love of melodrama and burlesque was long-standing. Samuel Butler, a leading actor of the company, was once heckled so fiercely during a performance of *Macbeth* that he interrupted his performance and danced the Lancashire Clog Hornpipe to placate the audience, who wanted more action!

Manager George Preston was succeeded by Frederick 'Barney' Egan in 1853. This was a period of mounting competition following the opening of the third Theatre Royal, Peter Street in 1845 and the Prince's Theatre in 1864. The successes of later stars including Charles Dillon and Edward Askew Sothern maintained the theatre's popularity, but it was too small to make an adequate return. The final run of performances were of the pantomime *Little Boy Blue*. After this, Egan was given a benefit with performances of *As You Like It* and *Much Ado About Nothing*.

This historic theatre's long and turbulent history finally came to an end on 16th March 1869, after which its doors closed forever. When the building was demolished some months later, the spring after which Spring Gardens was named was found some fifteen feet beneath the stage.

THEATRE ROYAL

Fountain Street

Opened: 1807
Closed: 1844

Following the loss of the Royal Patent in 1807, the first Theatre Royal ceded its status to the theatre in Fountain Street. Manchester's second Theatre Royal was opened on 29th June 1807, with the comedy *Folly as it Flies* and *Rosina*. The building, occupying a large site of 2,065 square yards, was bounded on the north by the Garrick's Head, on the east by Back Mosley Street, on the south by Charlotte Street and on the west by Fountain Street. The money was raised through a subscription, attracting the support of some of the most influential families in the town. The architect was Thomas Harrison. The theatre box lobby was, according to Mrs Linnaeus Banks, "so capacious that a coach and four could have been driven from one end to the other".

It was the very size of the theatre that apparently caused the first manager, Macready, so many problems. The annual rent amounted to £1,600 increased by rates and taxes to £2,200. The closure of the first Theatre Royal had been due in part because it was considered too small for the town's growing population, but it soon became apparent that the new theatre was too large. Plans were put in hand to reduce its size: the lobby being converted into a warehouse which divided the theatre from the Garrick's Head. Even so, the

Meeting celebrating Parliamentary Reform held in the Theatre Royal, Fountain Street, 1832.

theatre was still large enough to accommodate 2,000. Initially, seat prices were: lower boxes – four shillings, upper boxes – three shillings, pit – 2s 6d, gallery – one shilling. The smaller theatre proved more successful, the rent being reduced to £800 and the warehouse generating £300 in revenue. When Macready's partner, Galindo, withdrew, he called his son away from Rugby to take up the reins of management at the tender age of sixteen. William Charles Macready would put this early experience with his father to good use later on in life, when he became one of the central figures of Victorian theatre, both in Britain and abroad.

Apart from dramatic performances, the Theatre Royal offered opera and even equestrian events. When Macready the elder finally failed, the theatre passed into the hands of Robert Elliston, then Ward. Many actors were to make their mark at the theatre. John Vandenhoff "the noblest Roman of them all" became a fixed star, supported by such worthies as Thomas Cooper, Bass and Mrs M'Gibbon, Kemble, Mrs Garrick and Miss Booth. Joseph Grimaldi, the most famous of all pantomime clowns, also appeared at the theatre, as did John Astley and his equestrian troupe. Under the management of Anderson, the theatre vacillated between good and poor performances. Well-received productions included *Money*, which proved popular, featuring G.V. Brooke, Miss Julia Bennett and Miss Cleaver in principal roles.

On 24th December 1842, John Knowles, the new lessee, opened a redecorated and refurbished theatre. Under Knowles, the theatre enjoyed a short but significant revival. His company became one of the most renowned in the country, with members such as Samuel Butler, famed for his performances in *The School of Reform* and *As You Like It*. In 1843, new recruits included Emmeline Montague (later Mrs Compton) and John Sims Reeves – "a somewhat nervous young vocalist of swarthy complexion and rather uncouth appearance", who made his first appearance in *Tom Tug*.

The last two seasons at the Theatre Royal were to be the most successful in its history. But in the early hours of 7th May 1844, the theatre burned down. The initial cost of the building had been £10,700, but it was insured for £15,200. The insurance companies made a cash settlement, and Knowles decided to build a new theatre in Peter Street. However, in the interim performances continued as Knowles transferred the company to the Athenaeum, and later into Cooke's Circus in Mount Street.

THEATRE ROYAL

Peter Street

Opened: 1845

Closed: 1921

John Knowles employed Francis Chester and John Gould Irwin as the architects for his new theatre. Having studied the designs of London theatres they produced an impressive building dominated by two lofty Corinthian columns, that

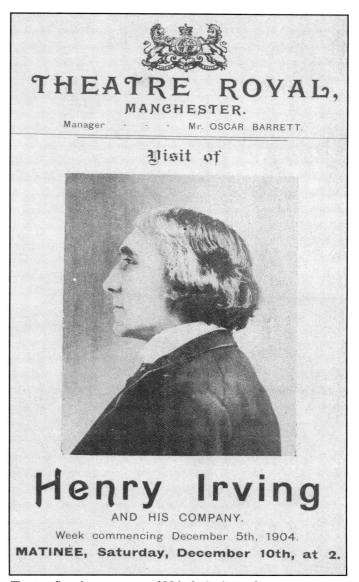

Theatre Royal programme, 1904: Irving's performances included The Merchant of Venice and The Bells.

confirmed Peter Street as one of the town's most important thoroughfares. The foundation stone was laid in December, 1844, and, after some delays, the theatre was opened on 29th September 1845. Appropriately for a theatre dedicated to Shakespeare, Knowles installed a Carrara marble statue of the playwright above the entrance. The erection of Manchester's first outdoor statue was relatively easy and cheap for the cost-conscious Knowles as his other business ventures included the running of a marble works. In total the building cost some £23,000 to erect, a price that included a massive water tank on the roof to help in the case of fire.

The new Theatre Royal quickly established itself as part of the cultural life of the town though not all patrons were pleased with Knowles's use of the stock company. There were memorable performances from outside companies. Probably none were more star-studded than the performance of *Every Man in His Humour* in July, 1847 whose cast included not only England's finest living novelist (Charles Dickens) and humorist (Douglas Jerrold) but also, in minor

Theatre Royal programme, March 1882. The main production was The Lancashire Witches.

However the takings from the occasional block-buster could not conceal the loss of custom to the new theatres and music halls that were opening in both the city-centre and the suburbs during the late Victorian and Edwardian years. The rise of the cinema soon posed another threat. In 1921, having recently been purchased by Raymond Pollock, the curtain came down on live entertainment at the Theatre Royal. Shortly afterwards it reopened as a cinema. For the next half-century, a number of different owners struggled to operate the building as a profitable cinema. Efforts were also made to convert it to other uses. Unrealised plans included in the post-war years the idea of turning it into a civic theatre, and in the 1960s the less imaginative scheme of replacing it with an office block. In 1972 cinema ended, and the building took on a new lease of life as a bingo hall. More recently, the building's acoustics have been tested by dance music, following its conversion into a discotheque, adding a further tableau to what some may wish to depict as the Royal's Progress.

TIVOLI THEATRE OF VARIETIES

See Alexandra Music Hall.

parts the country's most gifted caricaturist (George Cruikshank) and cartoonist (John Leech). The Royal's pantomimes were also well received. In 1859 Charles Calvert began his productions at the theatre to much critical acclaim. In the early 1860s Henry Irving was numbered among the members of the stock company, taking away from Manchester an understanding of his craft and friendships that were to serve him in subsequent years. Knowles's connection with the theatre ended in 1875. In the same year the auditorium was partially remodelled by Edward Salomons. Over the following decades the theatre was operated by a number of managers, including John Duffield and John Lawton. Selecting the right play remained a constant concern, though the visit of a good London company usually boosted audience levels. The Carl Rosa Opera Company, who had first appeared at the theatre in 1873, guaranteed good houses during their regular visits to Manchester. Surviving programmes record appearances by Sarah Bernhardt, Lily Langtry and Fred Terry. In 1895 Herbert Tree presented the premiere of, what was to become his most celebrated production, *Trilby*. Tree took the role of Svengali in this adaptation of George Du Maurier's famous novel. In April 1897, Manchester opera-lovers were the first to hear the seductive melodies of *La Bohème* in English, attended by Puccini. The appearance of star names, as when Dan Leno appeared in 1898, usually meant an increase in admission prices and the suspension of the "free list". Underlining their contribution to the theatre's overall profitability, pantomimes became even more spectacular.

Theatre Royal programme, Christmas pantomime 1900: Little Red Riding Hood.

UNIVERSITY THEATRE

Devas Street

Opened: 1965

Designed by the Building Partnership the University Theatre was one of the first purpose-built theatres to be opened in Manchester since the War. It was fitted into a small and difficult site on the then expanding campus of the Victoria University of Manchester. If externally undistinguished, inside the design of the stage and auditorium was advanced allowing a variety of what were called "actor-audience relationships". The maximum audience was 360 people. It was home to the University's Department of Drama but it was also regarded as a bridge between the university and the town. The theatre was officially opened by Dame Sybil Thorndike who predictably recalled the Gaiety years when Manchester had briefly become a theatrical principal rather than an a supporting player. The new theatre's first production, *The Shaughraun*, the work of the Victorian dramatist and actor Dion Boucicault, also looked back.

The theatre gradually settled down offering both new and tested dramas, developing its presence in the cultural life of the city. The Century Theatre, a mobile company formed in 1955, gave its first professional performance at the University Theatre on 26th October 1965 with Molière's *The Miser*. The company was originally based in Keswick. Its origins were in the work of John Ridley and Wilfred Harrison who set out to bring theatre to theatre-less towns, giving performances from a folding aluminium theatre. It enjoyed three successful years at the University Theatre, with notable performances by a host of up-and-coming actors including Tony Anholt, Warren Clarke, Tom Courtenay, Derek Fowlds, Denis Lill, Trevor Peacock and Anton Rodgers. The last performance given by the company was of *The Tempest* in June 1968, after which the company moved to Lancaster following the offer of a permanent theatre there.

Soon afterwards, the theatre became home to the 69 Theatre Company. The Company was the brainchild of three directors – Michael Elliott, Casper Wrede and Richard Pilbrow – reuniting them in the wake of their previous work together with the 59 Theatre Company at the Hammersmith Lyric. Century's former director, Braham Murray, also joined the company to form a quartet of directors with equal status. Beginning in 1968 the new company, suspicious of the metropolitan theatre world, used the theatre as the base from which to launch a theatrical project that in less than a decade saw them performing in their own theatre in the Royal Exchange. Among the many remarkable productions staged by the 69 Theatre Company was *Daniel Deronda,* of which one performance was disrupted by a bomb scare and the unscheduled appearance of a police inspector requesting the audience to "shout if you see anything suspicious". Fortunately, Vanessa Redgrave's electrifying performance as Gwendolen was only interrupted by applause at the appropriate time. After the 69 Theatre Company left, the theatre began what was to be a much longer association with the Contact Theatre Company.

Cover of booklet introducing the 69 Theatre Company to Manchester, 1968.

Manchester's young people's theatre company was established in 1972, following two years of negotiation between Manchester University and the Arts Council, North West Arts Association and Local Education Authorities. The project was initiated in May 1970 when the University Theatre Committee asked Hugh Hunt, Professor of Drama at Manchester University and Barry Sheppard, General Manager of the University Theatre, to compile a report on the long-term role and development of the theatre. They recommended that the University Theatre should be used as a theatre where a professional company of ten actors would perform plays which would encourage the appreciation of drama among young people. The company would present plays at the University Theatre for 21 weeks of the year and the rest of time would be spent in the community, performing in local schools, youth clubs and even on city streets.

The Arts Council gave the project an initial grant of £12,500 to set up the company. The name "Contact" was adopted to signify the links which the company intended to foster between young people and the theatre. The Contact Theatre Company began work on New Year's Day 1973, making it the third professional theatre company in Manchester, alongside the 69 Theatre Company and the Library Theatre Company. The immediate aim of the company was to make Contact Theatre "the Young Vic of the north west", with an emphasis on entertainment – rather than education – aimed at the 15-25 age group. These objectives were in line with the North West Arts Association's report *A New Stage.*

Under the management of Barry Sheppard, Bruce Huett and Paul Clements, the company began to present inventive and unpredictable productions. Early performances pulled no punches in exposing young audiences to serious and controversial social, political and moral issues. Paul

The Dresser premiered at the Royal Exchange in 1980.

Foster's *Tom Paine* was an early example. The first season continued this trend with productions of John Osborne's *Look Back in Anger* and Christopher Bond's *Downright Hooligan.*

The company established an early affinity with the works of Brecht, beginning with *The Caucasian Chalk Circle* in 1973. Other favourite modern writers included Samuel Beckett and Harold Pinter. New writing was also encouraged, including works by Alan Bleasdale, who was for a time the company's resident playwright, and Willy Russell.

In 1976 the company acquired a new administrative base. The Brickhouse, situated near the University Theatre in Devas Street, also included a small studio theatre which gave its own performances, beginning with David Rudkin's *Ashes* in November 1976. A notable attempt to cement the links between Contact and the community was *A Day in the Life of Manchester* (March 1978), in which a play was compiled from over 100 hours of recorded interviews with Manchester people.

Despite considerable success, both on the stage and in the community, Contact faced a funding crisis in 1982, following the university's withdrawal of financial support due to government imposed spending cuts. The company

struck back with a successful season which included Laurie Lee's *Cider with Rosie* and Dario Fo's *Accidental Death of an Anarchist*. Contact announced ambitious plans for the company to take total charge of the University Theatre and present a continuous professional season of 36 weeks, with a separate full-time touring company continuing with the company's community work. A children's theatre was also proposed.

Since that time, the company has continued to operate and has expanded its community work to provide performances and workshops for various groups in local schools, youth clubs, old people's homes, hospitals and play schemes. Sponsorship by local businesses including Manchester Airport and British Gas has helped to support the company's work in the face of mounting financial problems. Recent performances include *Troilus and Cressida*, *Dracula*, *Fall of the House of Usher* and *Three-penny Opera*, a continuation of the company's long and successful association with Brecht.

VICTORIA MUSIC HALL

Victoria Bridge

Opened: 1844

Ben Lang's Victoria Music Hall or Gallery was situated in the centre of Manchester near Victoria Bridge, or as its pass-out checks stated "near Manchester Old Church" (the Old Church became the Cathedral in 1847). It was part of a five storied building and capable, according to some reports, of holding some 2,000 people. In the 1850s the flat roof of the building previously used as a promenade was enclosed and used as a dance hall. It was a popular venue and attracted large crowds. Performers included Robert Reid, a comic singer and mimic, and John Millicent, a step dancer. As in all such businesses the money generated from the sale of refreshments was a major factor in determining the degree of profitability. Included in the drinks available to those attending the hall was Mrs. Lang's coffee, "moderate in price and unequalled in quality". Lang was nothing if not versatile and he also operated a workshop where it was said he worked on improving textile machinery.

In July 1868 Ben Lang's was the scene of Manchester's worst theatre disaster when an accident to a gas chandelier prompted a panic. In the ensuing rush to escape from the building 23 people, mostly teenagers, were killed and many more injured. Such tragedies were not uncommon in Victorian theatres, and they eventually led to the introduction of stricter regulations over the number, design and position of exits in public theatres and other places of entertainment.

WYTHENSHAWE FORUM THEATRE

See Forum Theatre.

PART THREE

Manchester Theatre Collection

Oxford Street, looking towards St. Peter's Square, June 1920.

THEATRE COLLECTION

I. REFERENCE WORKS

[1] Arnott, James Fullerton and John William Robinson. *English Theatrical Literature, 1559-1900: A Bibliography* [Incorporating Robert W. Lowe's A Bibliographical Account of English Theatrical Literature, published in 1888.] London: Society for Theatre Research, 1970.
792.0942 Ar7

[2] Baker, Blanch M. *Theatre and Allied Arts.* New York: Blom, 1967.
792 B185

[3] Banham, Martin. *Cambridge Guide to World Theatre.* Cambridge: Cambridge University Press, 1992. (New ed.)

[4] *British Alternative Theatre Directory.* Eastbourne: John Offord, 1979- [Ed. by Catherine Itzin et al.]
792 Br48

[5] Bryan, George B. *Stage Lives. A Bibliography Index to Theatrical Biographies in English.* Westport: Greenwood Press, 1985.
016.792 St2

[6] Busby, Roy. *British Music Hall: an Illustrated Who's Who from 1850 to the Present Day.* London: Elek, 1976.
792.7 Bu1

[7] Carpenter, Charles A. *Modern British Drama.* Arlington: AHM Publishing, 1979.

[8] Cavanagh, John. *British Theatre: a Bibliography 1901 to 1985.* Mottisfont: Motley Press, 1989.
Q016.792 Ca424

[9] Cheshire, David. *Theatre: History, Criticism and Reference.* London: Clive Bingley, 1967.
792 Ch7

[10] Conolly, L. W. and J. P. Wearing. *English Drama and Theatre, 1800-1900: a Guide to Information Sources.* Detroit: Gale Research, 1978.

[11] Esslin, Martin (ed.) *Illustrated Encyclopaedia of World Theatre.* London: Thames and Hudson, 1977.
Q792.0821 Il1

[12] Faxon, Frederick W. et al. (eds.) *Cumulated Dramatic Index, 1909-1949.* Boston: G.K. Hall, 1965.

[13] Hartnoll, Phyllis (ed.) *The Oxford Companion to the Theatre.* Oxford: Oxford University Press, 1983. (4th ed.) [First edition 1951; Second edition 1957; Third edition, 1967]
792.0321 Ha1

[14] Hartnoll, Phyllis and Peter Found (eds.) *The Concise Oxford Companion to the Theatre.* Oxford: Oxford University Press, 1992. (2nd ed.)
792.03 Co894

[15] Harwood, Ronald. *The Faber Book of the Theatre.* London: Faber and Faber, 1993.

[16] Herbert, Ian (ed.) *Who's Who in the Theatre.* 2 vols. Vol.1: *Biographies.* Vol.2: *Playbills.* Detroit: Gale, 1981.

[17] Howard, Diana. *Directory of Theatre Resources. A Guide to Research Collections and Information Services.* London: Library Association Services Group and The Society for Theatre Research, 1986. [2nd ed.]
QR792.0941 Di1

[18] Husbands, Peter G., ed. *Amateur Theatre in Great Britain: a Statistical Survey.* Banbury: Kemble, 1979.
Q792.0222 Hu1

[19] Johnson, Claudia D. and E. Vernon. *Nineteenth-Century Theatrical Memoirs.* Westport: Greenwood Press, 1982.

[20] Leacroft, Richard. *The Development of the English Playhouse: an Illustrated Survey of Theatre Building in England from Medieval to Modern Times.* London: Methuen, 1988.
725.822 Le7

[21] Link, Frederick M. *English Drama 1660-1800. A Guide to Information Sources.* Detroit: Gale Research, 1976.
LL016.822 Li1

[22] Loewenberg, Alfred. *The Theatre of the British Isles, excluding London: a Bibliography.* London: Society for Theatre Research, 1950.
792.0942 L1

[23] Mackintosh, Iain, and Michael Sell, eds. *Curtains!!!; or A New Life for Old Theatres.* Eastbourne: Offord in association with the Curtains!!! Committee, 1982. [. . . a complete gazetteer of all the surviving theatres, music halls of Great Britain . . .]
QR792.0941 Cu1

[24] Penninger, Frieda E. *English Drama to 1660 (excluding Shakespeare). A Guide to Information Sources.* Detroit: Gale Research, 1976. **822.09 Pe1**

[25] Pickering, David (ed.) *Dictionary of the Theatre.* London: Sphere, c1988.

[26] Stratman, Carl J. *Bibliography of Medieval Drama.* 2 vols. New York: Frederick Ungar, 1972.

[27] Stratman, Carl J. *Britain's Theatrical Periodicals 1720-1967. A Bibliography.* New York: New York Public Library, 1972. **QRA016.792 St1**

[28] Stratman, Carl J. et al. (eds.) *Restoration and Eighteenth-Century Theatre Research. A Bibliographical Guide 1900-1968.* Carbondale: Southern Illinois University Press, 1971.

[29] Wearing, J. P. *American and British Theatrical Biography: A Directory.* Metuchen, New Jersey and London: The Scarecrow Press, 1979. **QR792 We3**

[30] Whalon, Marion K. *Performing Arts Research. A Guide to Information Sources.* Detroit: Gale Research, 1976.

[31] *Who Was Who in the Theatre: 1912-1976. A Biographical Dictionary of Actors, Actresses, Directors, Playwrights and Producers of the English-speaking Theatre.* 4 vols. 1978. [Compiled from *Who's Who in the Theatre*, vol.1-15 (1912-1972).] **792.028 Wh1**

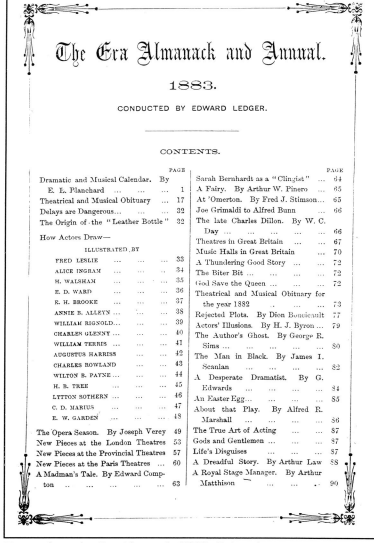

Extract from the Era Almanack (1883) listing theatres in Britain.

II. MANCHESTER THEATRES

ABRAHAM MOSS CENTRE THEATRE

[32]   Abraham Moss Centre Theatre, Manchester. *Annual Report-1984/5; Policy 1985/6.* Manchester: Manchester Education Committee, 1985.
ThQ792.094273 Ab1

APOLLO THEATRE

[33]   Manchester Apollo Theatre. *Handbills, playbills, leaflets.* 1983-. [Limited access]
Th792.094273 Ma287

[34]   Manchester Apollo Theatre. *Posters, 197-.*
ThF792.094273 Ma281

[35]   Manchester Apollo Theatre. *Theatre programmes* 1983-. [Limited access]
ThF792.094273 Ma288

BROADHEAD THEATRE CIRCUIT

[36]   Broadhead, W. H. *Broadhead Circuit Programmes, Manchester, 1901-1960.* 2 vols. Manchester, 1901-60. [Contents. Volume 1: Royal Osborne Theatre, Metropole Theatre, King's Theatre, Hulme Hippodrome, Grand Junction Theatre. Volume 2: The Playhouse, Queen's Park Hippodrome. Includes an illustrated pamphlet on the Royal Osborne Theatre Company, 1924. Incomplete.]
Th792.094273 Br1

[37]   Broadhead, W. H. *Plans and Elevations of Broadhead Theatres.* (photocopied plans). [n.d.]
ThF725.822 Br1

[38]   Manchester Public Libraries. Theatre Collection. *Chronological List of Programmes in the Collection: Broadhead Circuit, 1901-1960.* Manchester: Manchester Public Libraries, 197-. [Typescript]
Th792.094273 Ma164

[39]   Sharples, Robert. *The Broadhead Theatre Circuit: notes on a talk given by Mr. Robert Sharples.* Signed "W.A.H.", 2nd March 1951. 1951. [Photocopy of an article, with a carbon typescript note on the Manchester section of the Circuit.]
Th792.094273 Br2

[40]   Sharples, Robert. "The Broadhead Theatre Circuit" *Transactions of the North West Group, Society for Theatre Research* I (1951) 9-10.
Th792.09427 S1

CAPITOL THEATRE, DIDSBURY

[41]   Capitol Theatre, Manchester. *Souvenir of the Opening of the Capitol Theatre, Parrs Wood, Didsbury, May 21, 1931.* Manchester, 1931.
Q792.1 M18

CHORLTON REPERTORY THEATRE CLUB

[42]   Chorlton Repertory Theatre Club. *Programmes, October 1949-May 1953.* 4 vols. Manchester: Jackson & Co., 1949-53.
Th792.094273 Ch1

[43]   Chorlton Repertory Theatre Club, Manchester. *The Piccolo Theatre Company: Programmes, Spring season, 1954.*
Th792.094273 Ma737

[44]   Chorlton Repertory Theatre Club, Manchester. *Souvenir of the Two Hundredth Production, 1946-1950.* Manchester: Jackson & Co., 1950. [Title from cover. Also programme of "Ma's bit o'brass", by Ronald Gow, the play presented as the 200th production, 29th May-3rd June, 1950.]
Th792.094273 Ma51

COMEDY THEATRE

[45]   Comedy Theatre, Manchester. *Pantomime Books, 1886-1899.* Manchester, 1886-1899. [Contents: 1886: Little Red Riding Hood by Wilton Jones (E. Axon's copy with MS notes on cast). Manchester: Emmott & Co., 1886. Dick Whit-tington, by Wilton Jones (Ernest Axon's copy with MS notes). Manchester: John Heywood, 1887. Aladdin, by R. Newman (E. Axon's copy). Manchester: John Heywood, 1888. Cinderella, by William Wade (E. Axon's copy). Manchester: H. Darbyshire & Co., 1889. The Fair One with the Golden Locks, by William Wade. Manchester: Market Street Press, 1891. Goody Two Shoes, by William Wade. Manchester: The Market Street Press Works, 1893. Jack and Jill, by William Wade. Manchester: Butterworth & Co., 1894. Cinderella, by William Wade. Manchester: Market Street Press, 1895. Whittington and his Cat, by William Wade. Liverpool: The College Paper & Printing Co., 1897.]
Th792.094273 Ma73

[46]   Comedy Theatre, Manchester. *Playbills, 1891-1902.* [Incomplete]
Th792.094273 Ma115

[47]   Comedy Theatre, Manchester. *Programmes, 1885-1903.*
Th792.094273 Ma125

[48] Manchester Public Libraries. Theatre Collection. *Chronological List of Programmes in the Collection: Comedy Theatre, 1885-1903.* Manchester: Manchester Public Libraries, 197-. [Typescript]
Th792.094273 Ma165

FIRST EXCHANGE, MANCHESTER

[49] Exchange Theatre, Manchester. *Fragment of "Recruiting Officer" playbill.* 1743. [Limited access]
ThF792.094273 Ma194

[50] Exchange Theatre, Manchester. *Playbills, c.1750-1858.*
ThF792.094273 Ma196

FREE TRADE HALL

[51] Dudley, R., artist. *Scene from "The Frozen Deep", Act 2. Sketched in the Free Trade Hall, Manchester, August 28, 1857.* 1857. [The cast included Charles Dickens, Wilkie Collins and Augustus Egg.]
ThF792.094273 Du1

[52] Free Trade Hall, Manchester. *Programmes.* Manchester, 1863-. [Contents include programmes from Free Trade Hall, Gentlemen's Concert Hall, Midland Theatre, Town Hall.]
.094273 Ma145

[53] Manchester Corporation. City Architects Department. *Reconstruction of the Free Trade Hall.* Manchester, 1951. [for the information of the press]
ThF725.83 Ma5

GAIETY THEATRE

[54] ABC Television, Ltd. *The Curtain Goes Up: A.B.C. Television pays tribute to Miss Annie Horniman who, 50 years ago, started the first British Repertory at the Gaiety Theatre, Manchester.* [Script of a television transmission from the Library Theatre, Manchester, on September 14th, 1958.]
ThF792.0942 Ho12

[55] Aston, Elaine. "The 'New Woman' at Manchester's Gaiety Theatre" in Viv Gardner and Susan Rutherford (eds.), *The New Woman and her Sisters. Feminism and the Theatre, 1850-1914.* Hemel Hempstead: Harvester, 1992.
792.082 Ne996

[56] Gaiety Theatre, Manchester. *Alphabetical List of Plays Performed by Miss Horniman's Company 1907-1917.* 4v. in 1. [191-.] [Contents: September 23rd, 1907-December 31st, 1913. September 23rd, 1907-December 31st, 1914. September 23rd, 1907-

December 31st, 1915. September 23rd, 1907-June 30th, 1917.]
Th792.094273 Ma20

[57] Gaiety Theatre, Manchester. *Alphabetical list of plays performed by Miss Horniman's Company from September 23rd, 1907, to December 31st, 1916.* [191-.]
792.4273 M14

[58] Gaiety Theatre, Manchester. *Alphabetical list of plays performed by Miss Horniman's Company, with first dates [1907-1912].* 1912.
Th792.094273 Ma40

[59] Gaiety Theatre, Manchester. *Annual,* ed. by Henry Austin. Manchester: John Heywood & Sons, Ltd., 1909-11. [1909 issued title is *Gaiety Theatre Christmas Annual*]
Th792.094273 Ma21

[60] Gaiety Theatre, Manchester. *Goody Two Shoes: J. Pitt Hardacre's fourth . . . pantomime: [book of words],* 1893.
792.094273 Ma1

[61] Gaiety Theatre, Manchester. *Miss Horniman's Company and the Gaiety Theatre, Manchester in a repertoire of plays.* Stockport: Hurst Brothers, 1908. [Title from cover]
Th792.4273 M12

[62] Gaiety Theatre, Manchester. *Photographs and Caricatures of Miss Horniman and Members of her Company,* c.1908-12.
Th792.094273 Ma118

[63] Gaiety Theatre, Manchester. *Playbills, 1903-1915.*
Th792.094273 Ma117

[64] Gaiety Theatre, Manchester. *Portraits of Members of Miss Horniman's Company, taken from the "Christmas Annual" of 1909.* 1909.
792.094273 Ma23

[65] Gaiety Theatre, Manchester. *Programmes, 1904-1939.* 5 vols. 1904-39.
Th792.094273 Ma127

[66] Gaiety Theatre, Manchester. *Share receipts for travelling companies, 1906-1908.* 1906-8. [Manuscript]
MS792.094273 M6

[67] Horniman, Annie Elizabeth Fredericka. *Miss Horniman and the Gaiety Theatre. Photographs used to illustrate an exhibition held at Manchester Central Library.* Manchester: Manchester Public Libraries, 1978.
ThFF792.094273 Ho20

[68] Manchester Public Libraries. Theatre Collection. *Chronological List of Programmes in the Collection: Gaiety Theatre, 1904-1939.* 5 vols. Manchester: Manchester Public Libraries, 197-. [Typescript. Volume 1 includes a list of programmes from the Midland Hotel]
Th792.094273 Ma166

GENTLEMEN'S CONCERT HALL

[69] Manchester Public Libraries. Archives Department. *Printed Notices, Accounts and Plans of the Gentlemen's Concert Hall.* 1853-61.
MISC/324

GRAND THEATRE

[70] Grand Theatre, Manchester. *Programmes, including some Cinema Programmes, 1884-192-.* Manchester: Grand Theatre, 1884-192- [Includes the Grand Theatre, St. James's Hall, Leslie's Rusholme Pavilion.]
Th792.094273 Ma149

GREEN ROOM THEATRE

[71] Green Room Theatre, Manchester. *Photographs of Productions.* Manchester, 195-.
Th792.094273 Ma152

[72] Green Room Theatre, Manchester. *Playbills, 197-.* [Limited access]
ThF792.094273 Ma291

[73] Green Room Theatre, Manchester. *Playbills, Programmes and Miscellaneous Handouts, 1975-.* [Limited access]
ThF792.094273 Ma259

HORNIMAN THEATRE

[74] Manchester Polytechnic. School of Theatre. *Handbills, leaflets, etc.* 1983-. [Limited access]
ThF792.094273 Ma290

[75] Manchester Polytechnic. School of Theatre. *Playbills.* 1980- [Limited access]
ThF792.094273 Ma282

HULME HIPPODROME

[76] Hulme Playhouse. *Playbills.* 1955.
ThF792.094273 Hu5

[77] Hulme Playhouse. *Programmes.* 8/13 August 1955-.
792.0942 M13

LIBRARY THEATRE

[78] Coleman, Derek, ed. *Library Theatre, Manchester. The Resident Company Presents its 100th Production: "Never Had It So Good"; by John Wiles, [from] Tuesday 14th February 1961 until Saturday, 11th March 1961: Programme.* Manchester: Manchester Electric (Modern) Printing Co. Ltd., 1961. [Includes a list of plays presented from 1952-1961.]
Th792.094273 Ma274

[79] Friends of the Library Theatre Company. *Constitution.* Manchester, 1979.
ThF792.094273 Ma286

[80] Library Theatre, Manchester. *Acting Copies of Some Plays Produced at the Theatre During the Early 1960s.* Manchester, [n.d.]
Th792.094273 Ma202

[81] Library Theatre, Manchester. *Auditorium: Photographs.* Manchester, 1949-196-.
Th792.094273 Ma203

[82] Library Theatre, Manchester. "Central Library Theatre" *Manchester Review* 4 (1945-47) 228-31. [Contains an account of the Library Theatre's inaugural performance.]
017.442 M62

[83] Library Theatre, Manchester. *Cuttings.* Manchester, 1945-.
Th792.094273 Ma122

[84] Library Theatre, Manchester. *Display Cards listing Plays Performed by the Resident Company, 1952-1961.* Manchester, 1952-61.
Th792.094273 Ma124

[85] Library Theatre, Manchester. *Handbills.* 11 February 1947-. [irregular]
Th792.0942 M18

[86] Library Theatre, Manchester. *The Library Theatre's 200th Production: "In Celebration"; by David Storey, [from] Tuesday May 12 [1970]: Programme.* Manchester, 1970.
Th792.094273 Ma275

[87] Library Theatre, Manchester. *License for the public performance of stage plays (Annual).* 1947-8-. 1947-. [Limited access. Library wants 1950, 1959.]
ThF792.094273 Ma5

[88] Library Theatre, Manchester. *Photograph of Segovia and friends in Albert Square, on the occasion of Segovia's appearance in the Library Theatre,* 195-.
ThFF792.094273 Ma205

[89] Library Theatre, Manchester. *Photographs, 1954-1969*. Manchester, 1954-69. [Supplements the complete official photographic record "Productions" (Th792.094273 Ma120). Incomplete]
Th792.094273 Ma121

[90] Library Theatre, Manchester. *Photographs of Actors and Actresses*. Manchester, 196-.
Th792.094273 Ma123

[91] Library Theatre, Manchester. *Posters, produced by the Poster Artist, Manchester Public Libraries, 1952-1965*. Manchester, 1952-65.
ThFF792.094273 Ma119

[92] Library Theatre, Manchester. *Productions: Photographs of Actors and Décor, November 1952-*. Manchester, 1952-.
Th792.094273 Ma120

[93] Library Theatre, Manchester. *Programmes, etc.: Printing blocks. c.1950-69*. Manchester, 1950-69.
Th792.094273 Ma200

[94] Library Theatre, Manchester. *Programmes: September 30th 1946-*. 1946-.
Th792.094273 M1

[95] Library Theatre, Manchester, and Wythenshawe Forum Theatre. *List of performances and other events, 1982-*. 1982-
ThF792.094273 Ma284

[96] Manchester Public Libraries. Theatre Collection. *Chronological List of Programmes in the Collection: the Library Theatre*. v.1: 1943-1972. 197-. [Typescript]
Th792.094273 Ma172

[97] Mason, Bob. *Material relating to the production of Bob Mason's "Working Class Hero" at the Library Theatre, 22nd February-17th March 1984: posters, photographs and text of play*. 1984. [The play deals with the Peterloo uprising.]
FF942.733 Ma12

[98] Student Theatre. *Student Theatre (Once a Term)*. Leeds: Leeds University Union, 1964. [Includes an article by D.I. Colley, "Planning for success: the Manchester Library Theatre . . .".]
792.05 St4

LONDON GRAND MUSIC HALL

[99] London Grand Music Hall, Manchester. *The London Grand Music Hall, Bridge Street, Manchester*. Leeds: Charles Weldon, 1908. [Cover title: *A Reminiscence of Music Hall and Variety Entertainments, 1864-5-6*. A miniature reprint of an engagement and salary list of artists, kept by

Charles Weldon, the Manager, with an introduction by "H. J. D.", from the *Music Hall and Theatre Review*, 28th February, 1908.]
Th792.094273 Ma241

MANCHESTER HIPPODROME

[100] Hippodrome Theatre, Oxford Street and others. *Programmes, 1904-1961*. 2 vols. 1904-61. [Contents: Manchester Hippodrome, Oxford Street; Ardwick Empire, (Ardwick Green). [Incomplete]
Th792.094273 Ma43

[101] Hippodrome Theatre, Oxford Street, Manchester. *25th Anniversary: Opened 26th December 1904: 1904-1929*. Manchester, 1929.
Th792.094273 Ma47

[102] Hippodrome Theatre, Oxford Street, Manchester. *25th Anniversary: Opened 26th December 1904: 1904-1929: [souvenir programme]*. 1929.
Q792.094273 Ma295

[103] Hippodrome Theatre, Oxford Street, Manchester. *Opening performance, Boxing Day, December 26th, 1904, at 1.30 p.m. [souvenir programme]*. 1904. [One of a limited number printed on silk and presented to each of an invited audience.]
B.R.792.094273 Ma41

[104] Manchester Public Libraries. Theatre Collection. *Chronological List of Programmes in the Collection: Manchester Hippodrome (Oxford Street and Ardwick Green), 1904-1961*. Manchester: Manchester Public Libraries, 197-. [Typescript. See also New Manchester Hippodrome.]
Th792.094273 Ma167

MARSDEN STREET THEATRE

[105] Manchester Mercury. *A Selection of Items illustrating activity and interest in entertainment, Manchester 1752-June 1760*. 1752-60. [Includes lists of plays and players presented at "the theatre in Manchester". Typescript.]
B.R.F792.4273 M58

[106] Manchester Public Libraries. Theatre Collection. *Chronological List of Playbills in the Collection: Marsden Street Theatre, 1763-1770*. Manchester: Manchester Public Libraries, 197-. [Typescript]
Th792.094273 Ma163

[107] Marsden Street Theatre, Manchester. *Playbills, 1763-70*.
ThB.R.792.094273 Ma1

[108] Society for Theatre Research. North West Group. "Manchester's First Theatre: A Report of the North-West Regional Group of the Society for Theatre Research" *Manchester Review*, 7 (1955) 175-91.
017.442 M62

[109] Society for Theatre Research. North West Group. *Performances at "The Theatre, Manchester", i.e. the Marsden Street Theatre, 1760-1775, based on information in the Manchester Mercury; with selections of items of special interest from the Manchester Mercury March 1752-May 1775.* 1953. [Carbon typescript. Probably compiled by J. L. Hodgkinson, Chairman of the Society.]
ThF792.094273 So13

[110] Society for Theatre Research. North West Group. *The story of the first Manchester Theatre: a report.* 1954. [Typescript]
MS792.094273 S2

MINOR THEATRE

[111] Minor Theatre, Manchester. *Playbills, August 1815-October 1824.* Manchester, 1815-24.
Th792.094273 Ma108

[112] Royal Minor Theatre, Manchester. *Playbills, November 1828-January 1831.* Manchester, 1828-31.
Th792.094273 Ma108

NEW AMPHITHEATRE

[113] New Amphitheatre, Manchester. *Playbills.* 1809-14 [Incomplete]
Th792.094273 Ma108

NEW MANCHESTER HIPPODROME

[114] Hippodrome Theatre, Manchester. *Hippodrome Theatre, Ardwick Green. Playbills.* 1955-60. [Incomplete. See also Manchester Hippodrome.]
Th792.094273 Ma48

[115] Manchester Hippodrome. *Manchester Hippodrome, Ardwick Green, Manchester. Catalogue of the theatre furnishings, stage equipment, bar appointments, fixtures and general effects which will be sold at auction by F.S. Airey, Entwistle and Co. on the premises above on Wednesday, August 20th, 1961.* 1961.
Th792.094273 Ma271

NEW PAVILION THEATRE

[116] New Pavilion, Manchester. *Playbills.* 1825-26.
.094273 Ma108

NIA CENTRE

[117] Hulme Nia Centre. *Handbills, Leaflets, etc., 1991-* [Limited access]
Th792.094273 Hu297

OPERA HOUSE

[118] Howard & Wyndham Ltd. *The Opera House, Manchester 1912-1962: Golden Jubilee Souvenir.* Edinburgh: Howard & Wyndham, 1962.
ThQ792.094273 Ho4

[119] Manchester Public Libraries. Theatre Collection. *Chronological List of Programmes in the Collection: Opera House, 1912-1954.* Manchester, 197-. [Typescript]
Th792.094273 Ma168

[120] Manchester Public Libraries. Theatre Collection. *Chronological List of Performances at the Library Theatre, Opera House and Palace Theatre, Manchester.* 2 vols. Vol. 1: 1954-1964. Vol. 2: 1965-1972. 197-. [Typescript]
Th792.094273 Ma162

[121] Opera House, Manchester. *The Courier: Manchester's First Theatre House Organ.* Vol. 1, no. 1 May 1932, vol. 4, no. 1, Aug. 1936. Manchester: Whittaker & Robinson Ltd., 1932-6. [Official magazine of the Opera House, Manchester.]
ThQ792.094273 Co3

[122] Opera House, Manchester. *Fanfare. The Magazine of the Friends of the Manchester Opera House.* Vol. 1-4. Manchester: Friends of the Opera House, 1970-1.
Th792.094273 Ma143

[123] Opera House, Manchester. *Handbills and Miscellaneous Leaflets, 1929-.*
ThF792.094273 Ma265

[124] Opera House, Manchester. *New Manchester Theatre Limited: Prospectus.* Manchester, 1912.
Th792.094275 Ma96

[125] Opera House, Manchester. *Photographs of Productions.* 1916-59. [Contents: *As You Like It*, 1916. *Can-Can*, December 1945. *Oklahoma*, April, 1947. *Kismet*, December 1956. *The Love Doctor*, 1959.]
Th792.094273 Ma95

[126] Opera House, Manchester. *Playbills*. Manchester, 1948-57. [Also one bill for 27th December 1915.]
Th792.094273 Ma94

[127] Opera House, Manchester. *Press Releases*. *1984-*. 1984-. [Limited access]
ThF792.094273 Ma293

[128] Opera House, Manchester. *Programmes. 26 December 1912-*. Manchester, 1912-.
Th792.094273 Ma142

PALACE THEATRE

[129] Anglesey, Natalie. *Palace Theatre, Manchester*. Manchester: Pan Visuals, 1981.
Th792.094273 An1

[130] Cruikshank, Graeme. *The Palace Theatre 1891-1991: a Chronology*. Manchester: Palace Theatre, 1991.

[131] Manchester Palace of Varieties Ltd. Court of Chivalry. *Reports of Heraldic Cases in the Court of Chivalry, 1634-1707. Prepared from the records of the court; by G. D. Squibb*. Manchester: Private printing, bound in the Department of Printing and Photographic Technology, Manchester College of Technology, 1954. [Prepared for use at the hearing in December 1954 of the case of the Lord Mayor, Aldermen and Citizens of the City of Manchester v. the Manchester Palace of Varieties Ltd., being the first case to come before the court for over 200 years.]
929.8 C6

[132] Manchester Public Libraries. Archives Department. *Letters to Laurie Greig about purchase of land in Oxford Street for the Manchester Palace of Varieties*. 1889-92.
MISC/336

[133] Manchester Public Libraries. Theatre Collection. *Chronological List of Programmes in the Collection: Palace Theatre, 1891-1954*. 197-. [Typescript]
Th792.04273 Ma169

[134] Palace Theatre, Manchester. *Account Book*. 1908-11. [Copy of a film acquired by the Archives Department to complete a file of Palace Theatre account books (M359).]
MFTh792.094273 Ma279

[135] Palace Theatre, Manchester. *The Benevolent Flats Committee present an Evening with Johnny Mathis, Sunday, 7th March, 1971: Souvenir Brochure*. 1971.
ThQ792.094273 Ma278

[136] Palace Theatre, Manchester. *Chronological List of Performances, 1981-*. [Typescript]
ThF792.094273 Ma287

[137] Palace Theatre, Manchester. *Handbills and Miscellaneous Leaflets*. 1922-.
ThF792.094273 Ma266

[138] Palace Theatre, Manchester. *In the Presence of Her Majesty the Queen and HRH Prince Philip, Duke of Edinburgh, a Royal Gala Performance in aid of the Queen's Silver Jubilee Appeal, 20 June 1977: Programme*. Manchester, 1977.
ThQ792.094273 Ma251

[139] Palace Theatre, Manchester. *The Moscow Classical Ballet: Official Programme. With the star of the Bolshoi Ballet, Alla Tengizovna Khaniashvili*. London: Dewynters, 1988. [Limited access]
ThF792.094273 Ma097

[140] Palace Theatre, Manchester. *The Palace Theatre, Manchester, re-opening 18th March 1981*. Manchester: Palace Theatre, 1981.
ThQ792.094273 Ma277

[141] Palace Theatre, Manchester. *Pantomime Books*. Manchester: John Heywood, 1897. [Contents: 1897: Jack and Jill, by J. J. Dallas.]
Th792.094273 Ma77

[142] Palace Theatre, Manchester. *Photographs of Scenes from a Pantomime*. [n.d.]
Th792.094273 Ma78

[143] Palace Theatre, Manchester. *Playbills*. [Incomplete] 1957-67.
Th792.094273 Ma76

[144] Palace Theatre, Manchester. *Press Releases*. Manchester, 1980-.
ThF792.094273 Ma276

[145] Palace Theatre, Manchester. *Programmes. 8th June, 1891-*. Manchester, 1891-. [Incomplete. Includes North Manchester Amateur Operatic Society and North Cheshire Amateur Operatic Society programmes, 1967- and 1938- respectively.]
Th792.094273 Ma79

[146] Palace Theatre, Manchester. *Sky: live in '83:* [tour programme]. Latent Image Ltd, 1983.
ThF792.094273 Ma294

[147] Palace Theatre, Manchester. *Souvenir*. Manchester: E. Hulton & Co. Ltd (printers), 1913. [The pamphlet contains a description of the new Palace Theatre.]
Th792.094273 Ma38

PRINCE'S THEATRE

[148] Calvert, Charles Alexander. *Prince's Theatre, [Manchester. Extracts from the] London and Manchester Press [on] the Merchant of Venice*. With a preface by Charles Calvert. Manchester, 1871.
Th792.0942733 L275/5

[149] Calvert, Charles Alexander. *Shakespeare's Henry the Fifth, as produced under the direction of Charles Calvert, at the Prince's Theatre, Manchester: opinions of the press*. Manchester, 1872. [Other copies at 822.33 W3.9 and L295/2-3.]
Th792.094273 Ca5

[150] Humphreys, J. Norman. *Prince's Theatre, Manchester*. 1940. [Manuscript attributed to J. Norman Humphreys.]
Th792.094273 Hu1

[151] Manchester Public Libraries. Theatre Collection. *Chronological List of Programmes in the Collection: Prince's Theatre, 1864-1939*. 197-. [Typescript]
Th792.094273 Ma170

[152] O'Connor, Daniel S., ed. *Peter Pan Keepsake*. London: Chatto & Windus, 1907. [Includes references to Prince's Theatre, Manchester.]
ThQ792.094273 Pe1

[153] Prince's Theatre, Manchester. *Admission Tickets*. [n.d.] [Mounted on 3 sheets in portfolio]
Th792.094273 Ma46

[154] Prince's Theatre, Manchester. *Memorandum of Association and Articles of Association of the Prince's Theatre Co. Ltd*. 1868. [Two cuttings from periodicals on the subject of the management of the theatre, 1864-71, and an illustration of the interior.]
ThF792.094273 Ma45

[155] Prince's Theatre, Manchester. *Pantomime Books*. 3 vols. Contents:

Vol.1: 1864: Mother Goose; by Pyngle Layne. 1865: Little Bopeep; by Edward Robertson Ward. 1866: Robin Hood; by Edwin Waugh. 1867: Gulliver's Travels; by William Brough (also 2nd ed). 1869: Froggee would a Wooing Go; by William Brough. 1870: Harlequin Blackbird.

Vol.2: 1872: Forty Thieves. 1878: Puss in Boots. 1884: Ali Baba and the Forty Other Thieves. 1866: Robinson Crusoe; by Wm. Wade, with MS notes by E. Axon. 1887: Beauty and the Beast; by William Wade, with MS notes by E. Axon. 1888: Sinbad the Sailor; by George Dance, with MS notes by E. Axon. 1890: Little Bo-Peep; by George

Dance (two variant eds). 1894: Little Red Riding Hood; by Wilton Jones and Thos. W Charles.

Vol.3: 1895: Robinson Crusoe; by Wilton Jones and T. W. Charles. 1897: Puss in Boots; by John J. Wood. 1898: Sinbad the Sailor; by Jay Hickory Wood and A. M. Thompson. 1899: Cinderella. 1902: Robinson Crusoe; by A. M. Thompson and Robert Courtneidge. 1903: The Forty Thieves; by J. Hickory Wood. Manchester, 1864-1903.
Th792.094273 Ma83 and Ma83/A

[156] Prince's Theatre, Manchester. *Picture Postcards advertising productions, c.1900-1920*. 1900-20. [Limited access. Includes a few cards from other theatres.]
Th792.094273 Ma91

[157] Prince's Theatre, Manchester. *Playbills, 1865-1940*. Manchester, 1865-1940. [Incomplete]
Th792.094273 Ma90

[158] Prince's Theatre, Manchester. *Prince's Annual Season, 1876-7: illustrated account of the pantomime "Sinbad, or Harlequin Old Man of the Sea and the Diamond Fay of the Enchanted Valley of the Roc"*, c.1876.
Th792.094273 Ma85

[159] Prince's Theatre, Manchester. *The Prince's Theatre, Manchester: Agreement [with] Nora Johnston*. 1923. [Limited access. An agreement for the production of Maeterlinck's "The Blue Bird" by Nora Johnston's Company, 25th February-1st March 1924.]
B.R.792.094273 Ma11

[160] Prince's Theatre, Manchester. *The Prince's Theatre, Manchester: Agreement with Owen Nares*. 1924. [Limited access. An agreement for the production of a new play by Owen Nares and London Company, 3rd-8th November, 1924.]
B.R.F792.094273 Ma14

[161] Prince's Theatre, Manchester. *Programmes, 1864-1940*. [Incomplete. Supplemented by 7 bound volumes covering 1882-4, 1902, 1903, 1904, 1913, 1914 and 1927.]
Th792.094273 Ma130

[162] Prince's Theatre, Manchester. *A Souvenir of the Revival of Shakespeare's comedy "As You Like It" at the Prince's Theatre, Sept. 1902*. Manchester, 1902. [Contents: Thompson, A. M.: *A discursive history of the play*. Blatchford, R.: *An Appreciation of "As You Like It"*. Darbyshire, A.: *Some recollections of Helen Faucit's final appearance on the stage in the character of Rosalind*.]
822.33 O3.8

[163] Prince's Theatre, Manchester. *Stock Companies: interesting extracts from the press, including an account of Manchester Stock Companies, past and present.* Manchester: A. Ireland & Co. (printers), 1884. [Articles attributed by MS notes to J. Evans and W. T. Arnold.]
Th792.094273 Ma55

[164] Prince's Theatre, Manchester, and Manchester Theatre Royal. *Pantomime: illustrations of scenes extracted from various periodicals, 1874-84.*
Th792.0942 Ma87

[165] Shakespeare, William. *King Henry V. Shakespeare's historical play of Henry the Fifth, arranged... by Charles Calvert and produced at the Prince's Theatre, Manchester, September 1872.* Manchester, 1872.
822.33 W3.10

[166] Shakespeare, William. *A Midsummer Night's Dream. Notes by an Old Playgoer.* Manchester, 1901. [Souvenir of production at the Prince's Theatre.]
Th792.4273 P1

[167] The Story of Abomelique. *The Story of Abomelique, the (very!) married man; generally called Blue-beard; showing how a misrepresented individual got at least some justice done him at the Prince's Theatre.* 18–. [Verses published during the representation of Bluebeard pantomime at the Prince's Theatre, Manchester.]
Th792.0942733 L275/6

[168] Thompson, Fred & Son, Auctioneers. *Prince's Theatre, Manchester. Re Bernard, a bankrupt. [Sale catalogue of] scenery, properties, furniture dresses, works of vertu, & c.* Manchester, 1882.
L310/11

QUEEN'S THEATRE, SPRING GARDENS

[169] Broadbent, R. J. *The Old Queen's Theatre, Manchester.* Manchester, [n.d.] [Original kept in Liverpool Record Office MS Mq414. Microfilm copy.]
MF792.094273 Br3

[170] Queen's Theatre, Spring Gardens, Manchester. *Catalogue of the internal fittings and loose effects of the Queen's Theatre, to be sold by auction by Mr. Edward Harrison, Mar. 18th 1869.* Manchester: Cave & Sever (printers), 1869.
Th792.094273 Ma15

[171] Queen's Theatre, Spring Gardens, Manchester. *Pantomime Books.* Manchester, 1858-68. [Contents: 1858: Harlequin Green Beetle. 1860: Harlequin Aladdin; by J. H. Doyne. 1861: Harlequin Valentine and Orson; by J. H. Doyne. 1862: The Invisible Prince; by Frank Maitland. 1863: Harlequin Sinbad the Sailor; by Charles Horsman. 1864: Harlequin King Humpty Dumpty; by Wm. Seaman. 1865: Harlequin Whittington and his Cat. 1866: Harlequin and Kafoozalum; by J. H. Doyne. 1867: Harlequin Guy Fawkes. 1868: A Apple pie: and Little Boy Blue; or, Harlequin Jack-in-the-Box and the World of Toys; by Jas. Shepley. (Library wants 1859).]
Th792.094273 Ma80

[172] Queen's Theatre, Spring Gardens, Manchester. *Playbills, 1831-1869.* Manchester, 1831-69.
Th792.094273 Ma108

QUEEN'S THEATRE, BRIDGE STREET

[173] Bleackley, Edward Overall. *Real Life: an Original Comedy Drama in Four Acts.* Manchester: J. Heywood, 1872. [The author was a Manchester businessman. The play was produced at the Queen's Theatre, Manchester, in December 1872 and this copy is bound with programme, playbill, criticisms and a life of the author. Other copies of the text are shelved at 822.89 Bl1 and 822.8 B25.]
Th792.094273 Bl1

[174] Forsyth, J. J. B. *Queen's Theatre, Manchester. Grand Christmas Pantomime, 1879-80, entitled "Old Mother Goose".* Manchester, 1880.
792.0942733 L526/12

[175] Maltby, Alfred. *Queen's Theatre, Bridge Street, Manchester Grand Comic Christmas Pantomime of Robinson Crusoe.* Manchester, 1874-5.
Th792.0942733 L526/10

[176] Manchester Public Libraries. Theatre Collection. *Chronological List of Programmes in the Collection: Queen's Theatre, Bridge Street, Manchester, 1873-1911.* 197-. [Typescript]
Th792.094273 Ma171

[177] Queen's Theatre, Bridge Street, Manchester. *Souvenir of Mr. Richard Flanagan's Grand Elizabethan Production "Essex", by Alfred C. Calmour. Monday, October 7th 1907. Historical Note and Illustrations by William Palmer.* Manchester: G. Hargreaves (printer), 1907.
Th792.094273 Pa2

[178] Queen's Theatre, Bridge Street, Manchester. *Pantomime Books.* Manchester, 1870-1896. [Contents: 1870: Ali Baba and the Forty Thieves; by James Shepley. 1874: Robinson Crusoe; by Alfred Maltby. 1877: Jack and the Beanstalk; by J. J. B. Forsyth. 1879: Old Mother Goose; by J. J. B.

Forsyth. 1881: Aladdin; by J. T. Denny. 1882: Beauty and the Beast; by John F. McArdle. 1883: Little Red Riding Hood; by J. Wilton Jones. 1888: Blue Beard; by J. P. Taylor. 1889: Robinson Crusoe; by T. F. Doyle. 1893: Sinbad the Sailor; by T. F. Doyle. 1896: Red Riding Hood; by Eric J. Buxton.
Th792.094273 Ma82

[179] Queen's Theatre, Bridge Street, Manchester. *Playbills*. Manchester, 1876-1910. [Incomplete]
Th792.094273 Ma97

[180] Queen's Theatre, Bridge Street, Manchester. *Programme of "As You Like It"*. 1907.
ThQ792.094273 Ma255

[181] Queen's Theatre, Bridge Street, Manchester. *Programmes*. 1873-1911. [Incomplete]
Th792.094273 Ma134

[182] Queen's Theatre, Bridge Street, Manchester. *Souvenir of Mr. R. Flanagan's eighth Shakespearian revival, "Henry the Eighth". With an Introduction by Sir William Bailey*. Manchester: G. Hargreaves, 1903.
Th792.094273 Ma8

[183] Queen's Theatre, Bridge Street, Manchester. *Souvenir of Richard Flanagan's fourth Shakespearian revival, "The Winter's Tale", Jan. 21st 1899*. Title from cover. Manchester: John Heywood, 1899.
Th792.094273 Ma253

[184] Queen's Theatre, Bridge Street, Manchester. *Souvenir of Mr. R. Flanagan's ninth Shakespearian revival, "Richard the Third"*. Manchester: G. Hargreaves, 1903.
ThQ792.094273 Ma254

[185] Queen's Theatre, Bridge Street, Manchester. *Souvenir of Mr Richard Flanagan's tenth Shakespearian revival, "Romeo and Juliet", Queen's Theatre, Manchester ... 1905*. Manchester: G. Hargreaves, 1905.
ThF792.094273 Ma66

[186] Queen's Theatre, Bridge Street, Manchester. *Souvenir of Mr. Richard Flanagan's eleventh Shakespearian revival, Cymbeline, Queen's Theatre, Manchester, 1906*. Manchester: George Hargreaves (printer), 1906.
ThF792.094273 Ma636

[187] Queen's Theatre, Bridge Street, Manchester. *Souvenir of Mr. R. Flanagan's twelfth Shakespearian revival, "Othello"*. Manchester: G. Hargreaves, 1907.
ThQ792.094273 Ma256

[188] Thompson, Fred & Son, Auctioneers. *Queen's Theatre, Manchester: expiration of lease: [Sale Catalogue]. March 23 and 24*. Manchester, 1885.
L310/12

QUEEN'S THEATRE, BRIDGEWATER STREET

[189] New Queen's Theatre, Bridgewater Street, Manchester. *New Queen's Theatre (Manchester) Limited: Prospectus*. Manchester: G. Hargreaves (printer), 1911. [The project for a theatre in Bridgewater Street was abandoned and superseded by the New Manchester Theatre, Quay Street, later the Opera House. Also contains an application form for 35,000 shares of £1 each. Pamphlet-typed contract.]
Th792.094273 Ma98

ROYAL EXCHANGE THEATRE

[190] Fraser, David, ed. *The Royal Exchange Theatre Company: An Illustrated Record*. Manchester: Royal Exchange Theatre Company Ltd., 1988.
ThQ792.094273 Ro2

[191] Gilbert, W. Stephen. "Two Stages Forward: W. Stephen Gilbert looks at new theatres in Manchester and Leicester". *Plays and Players* (December 1973) [Article covering the Royal Exchange Theatre, Manchester and the Haymarket Theatre, Leicester.]
ThF792.09427 Gi1

[192] Mayer, David. "Fair Royal Exchange: David Mayer visits Manchester's new theatre and reviews "The Rivals" and "The Prince of Homburg". *Plays and Players* (November 1976).
ThF792.094273 Ma273

[193] Royal Exchange Theatre, Manchester. "A Dramatic Exchange". *Architects' Journal* 163 (28th January 1976) 158-60.
ThF792.094273 Dr1

[194] Royal Exchange Theatre, Manchester. *Handouts, Forthcoming Attractions, etc*. Manchester, 1976-.
Th792.094273 Ma262

[195] Royal Exchange Theatre, Manchester. *Miscellaneous Leaflets: post-opening*. Manchester, 1976-. [Includes press releases]
Th792.094273 Ma245

[196] Royal Exchange Theatre, Manchester. *Playbills, 1973-*. Manchester, 1973-. [Incomplete]
Th792.094273 Ma282

[197] Royal Exchange Theatre, Manchester. *Programmes.* 1976-.
ThF792.094273 Ma264

[198] Royal Exchange Theatre, Manchester. *Report of the Chairman (Annual), 1978-79.* 1980.
ThQ792.094273 Ma272

[199] The Royal Exchange Theatre News. *The Royal Exchange Theatre News: the quarterly newspaper of the Royal Exchange Theatre Company.* 1980.
ThF792.094273 Ro1

[200] Scott, R. D. H. *The Biggest Room in the World: A Short History of the Manchester Royal Exchange.* Manchester: Royal Exchange Theatre Trust, 1976.
380 Sc1

[201] Stage Exchange. *Stage Exchange: The Royal Exchange Theatre, Manchester.* 1976.
ThF792.094273 St1

[202] Williams, Michael. *At the Court of King Cotton.* The Royal Exchange Theatre, Manchester. 1977. [Photocopied extract from "Tabs", Spring 1977.]
ThF792.094273 Wi5

ROYAL NORTHERN COLLEGE OF MUSIC OPERA HOUSE

[203] Royal Northern College of Music Opera House, Manchester. *Handbills, etc. 1973-.* 1973-. [Incomplete]
Th792.094273 Ma190

[204] Royal Northern College of Music Opera Theatre, Manchester. *Playbills.* 1974-.
ThF792.094273 Ma268

RUSHOLME THEATRE

[205] Manchester Repertory Theatre Ltd. *Playbills.* Manchester, 1934-40.
Th792.094273 Ma104

[206] Manchester Repertory Theatre Ltd. *Programmes.* 3 vols. Manchester, 1925-40. [Incomplete. Known as the Rusholme Theatre, the New Manchester Repertory Theatre, and Manchester Repertory Theatre, Rusholme.]
Th792.094273 Ma37

[207] Manchester Repertory Theatre Ltd. *Share Certificate, 1935; and Report and Accounts for the Year ended 31st May 1938.* Manchester, 1938.
Th792.094273 Ma103

[208] Rusholme Theatre, Manchester. *Reception by the Lord Mayor and Lady Mayoress (Councillor and Mrs. R. Noton Barclay) to meet the directors, management and repertory players of the Rusholme Theatre [at the] Town Hall, Manchester [on] 21 July 1930. Programme.* Manchester: A. & S. Walker (printer), 1930.
Th792.094273 Re182

ST JAMES'S THEATRE

[209] St James's Theatre, Manchester. *Pantomime Books, 1886-1898.* Manchester, 1886-98. [Contents: 1866: Aladdin; by J. Swift. (Ernest Axon's copy.) 1895: Cinderella; by John J. Sullivan. 1898: The Babes in the Wood; by Eric J. Buxton.]
Th792.094273 Ma81

[210] St James's Theatre, Manchester. *Playbills, June-July, 1884.* Manchester, 1884.
Th792.094273 Ma100

STABLES THEATRE

[211] McDougal, Gordon. *Stables Theatre Club.* [c.1970]
Th792.094273 Ma269

[212] Stables Theatre Club, Manchester. *Playbills, Miscellaneous Leaflets, etc.* Manchester, 1969-.
Th792.094273 Ma209

THEATRE ROYAL, SPRING GARDENS

[213] [Anon.] The Theatrical Inquisitor. *The Theatrical Inquisitor; or an enquiry into what two worthy managers have promised and what performed.* Manchester: R. & W. Dean & Co., 1804.
Th792.094273 Th12

[214] *The Argus; or, the Theatrical Observer, containing critical, yet impartial, strictures on the merits and demerits of the principal performers of the Theatre Royal, Manchester.* Manchester: R. & W. Dean, 1804-5. [6 numbers: No. 1, 24th Nov 1804-No. 6, 30 Mar 1805. Library wants no. 3.]
Th792.094273 Ar3

[215] *Argus's Answer to the Historian Mr. Huddart; addressed to the inhabitants of Manchester.* Manchester: R. & W. Dean & Co., 1804.

[216] Benwell, J. M. *An Essay on the danger of unjust criticism. By J. M. Benwell, of the Theatre Royal, Manchester. Occasioned by a publication entitled The Thespian Review.* Manchester: Wardle (printer), 1806.

[217] Candid [pseud.] *Impartial Reflections, on the conduct of the managers, and merits of some of the performers of the Theatre-Royal, Manchester. With observations on a late publication, entitled "A Peep into the Theatre".* Manchester: W. Shelmerdine & Co., 1800.

[218] Candid [pseud.] *A Letter to Mr. Ward, one of the Managers of the Theatre at Manchester occasioned by intemperate charge of malice and malignity against the writer of "Impartial Reflections".* Manchester: G. Bancks, 1800.
Th792.094273 Ca3

[219] *The Censor; or, Theatrical Review; by a candid observer.* Nos. 1-2. Manchester: M. Wardle (printer), 1807.
Th792.094273 Ce1

[220] Cross, William. *An Expostulatory Address to the Public. By William Cross of the Theatre-Royal, Manchester.* Manchester: W. Cowdroy; B. Hopper, 1800. [On the reception . . . lately experienced, from some of the frequenters to the Manchester Theatre.]
Th792.094273 Cr1

[221] Lavish, Charles. *Letter to the proprietors of the Theatre Royal, Manchester.* Manchester, 1800.

[222] Manchester Public Libraries. Archives Department. *Act of Parliament to Enable His Majesty to Licence a Playhouse in Manchester.* 1775.
L1/55/5/13

[223] Manchester Public Libraries. Archives Department. *Agreement of rope dancers and tumblers to perform for eight weeks at the Theatre Royal.* 1785.
M/C 118

[224] Manchester Public Libraries. Archives Department. *Grant of a Share in the Theatre to be Built at Spring Gardens.* 1775.
M/C 117

[225] *Manchester Songster: a collection of the most favourite songs that have been sung at the public places of entertainment in London and at the Theatre-Royal, Manchester.* Manchester, 1792.
821.04 M25

[226] Manchester Theatre. *An Act for enabling His Majesty to license a Playhouse in the town of Manchester, in the County Palatine of Lancaster.* London: Charles Eyre & William Strahan, 1775.
ThF792.094273 Ac1

[227] Observator [pseud.] *Critical review of the conduct of the managers, with observations on some of the performers of the Theatre Royal.* Manchester, 1803.
Th792.094273 Ca3/2

[228] Pogson, Rex. *The First Theatre Royal, 1775-1807.* 1960. [Author's carbon typescript, published as part 2 of Hodgkinson and Pogson's *The Early Manchester Theatre* (ThF792.094273 Ho3/ Th792.094273 Ho1)]
MSQ792.094273 Po1

[229] Theatre Royal, Manchester. *A Peep into the Theatre-Royal, Manchester: with some remarks on the merits and demerits of the performers.* Manchester: G. Bancks, 1800. (2nd ed.)
Th792.4273 T7

[230] Theatre Royal, Manchester. *Lines Spoken in the Theatre Royal Manchester by Mr. Young, 9 January 1806, the evening of the internment of the remains of the lamented Vice-Admiral Lord Viscount Nelson . . . by the author of the Manchester Guide.* Manchester, 1806.
792.094273 f 1806/4 M/cr

[231] Theatre Royal, Manchester. *Catalogue of various articles to be sold by auction, at the Theatre Royal, Manchester, on Monday, 31st July, 1809.* Manchester, 1809.
792.0942733 H442/1

[232] Theatre Royal, Manchester. *Playbills.* Manchester, 1778-1921. [Incomplete]
Th792.094273 Ma105

[233] *The Thespian Review: an examination of the merits and demerits of the performers on the Manchester Stage.* No. 1, 1st Feb. 1806-No. 7, 15th March 1806. Manchester: J. Aston, 1806.
Th792.094273 Th8

[234] *The Townsman.* 1803-5.
Th792.094273 To1

[235] Ward, J. M. *The History of the Theatre Royal, Manchester, 1775-1922.* 1973. [Typescript]
Th792.094273 Wa1

[236] Watson, James, poet and librarian. *An Address to the Inhabitants of Manchester on Theatricals; by a Townsman.* In verse. No. 1-3 in 2 vols. Manchester: G. Bancks (printer), 1803.
Th792.094273 To4/To1

[237] Winston, James. *Theatre Royal, Manchester.* 1805. [Taken from *The Theatric Tourist*, pp. 61-2, photographic copy, positive of p. 63, and coloured plate.]
ThF792.094273 Wi1

THEATRE ROYAL, FOUNTAIN STREET

[238] Anderson, J. H., and W. J. Hammond. *Account Book of Receipts and Expenditure for the Theatre Royal, Manchester, 8th Dec. 1841-10th Sept. 1842, and for the Theatre Royal, Liverpool, 8 Dec. 1841-4 Nov. 1842*. Manuscript. 1841-2.
MSF792.4272 A1

[239] Manchester Public Libraries. Archives Department. *Letters Patent to Licence Playhouse*. 1817.
M/C 972

[240] Manchester Public Libraries. Archives Department. *Seating Plan at Theatre Royal for dinner for J. Thomas Hope, Parliamentary Candidate*. 1832.
MISC/122

[241] Manchester Public Libraries. Archives Department. *Seating Plan of dinner for the Duke of Wellington held in Theatre, Fountain Street*. 1830.
M71/2/18/6

[242] Manchester Public Libraries. Archives Department. *Share in the Theatre in Fountain Street and in Letters Patent Licencing it, assigned by Marriage Settlement*. 1823.
M/C 974

[243] Manchester Public Libraries. Archives Department. *Share of Thos. Faulkner Phillips in the Manchester Theatre Royal Bequeathed in his Will*. 1822.
M/C 973

[244] Manchester Public Libraries. Archives Department. *Warrant for drawing up Letters Patent to Licence a Playhouse for 21 Years*. 1816.
M/C 119

[245] Theatre Royal, Manchester. *Second Grand Miscellaneous Concert on Wednesday evening, October the 30th 1811, in the Theatre Royal, under the direction of Mr Yaniewicz*. 1811. [Limited access]
Th791 M19

THEATRE ROYAL, PETER STREET

[246] Calvert, Charles Alexander. *Calvert Memorial Performance, Theatre Royal, Manchester, 1st and 2nd October, 1879*. Manchester: G. Falkner & Son, 1879.
ThQ792.094273 Ca1

[247] *Manchester Observer: Issued daily in connection with the Theatre Royal; containing the programmes, press criticisms, miscellaneous notes, and advertisements*. 12 vols: No. 1, 17th Apr 1865-No. 2903, 27th Mar 1875. Manchester: Thomas Chambers, 1865-75.
F792.4273 M6

[248] Manchester Public Libraries. Archives Department. *Draft letter from Dr. Edmund Lyon to a newspaper, criticising the choice of play at the Patent Theatre*. [c.1850]
M134/5/4/2

[249] Manchester Public Libraries. Theatre Collection. *Chronological List of Programmes in the Collection: Theatre Royal, 1861-1923*. 6 vols., 197-. [Typescript]
Th792.094273 Ma173

[250] Theatre Royal, Manchester. *Pantomime Books*. 2 vols. Contents:

Vol.1: 1808: Harlequin and Mother Goose. (Title page bears MS note, "By Thomas Dibdin, 1808". MS note on p.iii "Produced at the Theatre Royal, Fountain St, under Bradbury's direction, February 1st, 1808). 1846: The Devil to Pay. 1847: Harlequin Jack the Giant Killer, (2nd ed.) 1848: Harlequin Sindbad, the Sailor; by C. A. Somerset, (3rd ed.) 1849: The Mistletoe Bough, (4th ed.) 1851: Harlequin and the Babes in the Wood, (9th ed.) 1854: Jack and the Beanstalk, (11th ed.) 1856: Forty Thieves. 1857: Robinson Crusoe. 1858: Robin Hood, (16th ed.) 1859: Blue Beard, (12th ed.) 1860: Cinderella, (19th ed.) 1861: Beauty and the Beast, (3rd & 17th eds.) 1862: The House that Jack Built, (4th & 19th eds.) 1863: The Sleeping Beauty; by T. Chambers and W. S. Hyde, (20th ed.) 1864: Puss in Boots; by T. Chambers and W. S. Hyde, (25th ed.) 1868: Valentine & Orson. 1869: Sindbad the Sailor, by John Strachan jun.

Vol.2: 1886: Blue Beard. (MS note on p.i, by E. Axon "Book by T. F. Doyle".) 1887: Old Mother Goose and the Sleeping Princess; (by T. F. Doyle. E. Axon's copy, with MS notes). 1888: The forty Thieves; by T. F. Doyle. 1889: Dick Whittington; by George Dance. (Ernest Axon's copy). 1890: Aladdin; by Horace Lennard. 1892: Little Red Riding Hood, Bonnie Boy Blue [etc.]; by Fred Locke. 1893: Babes in the Wood; or, Harlequin Robin Hood; by Fred Locke. 1894: Sindbad the Sailor; by Fred Locke. 1896: Cinderella. 1897: Aladdin. 1898: The Babes in the Wood. 1901: Jack and the Beanstalk; by A. H. Smith. 1904: Mother Goose; by J. Hickory Wood [and] William Wade. Manchester, 1808-1904.
Th792.094273 Ma86

[251] Theatre Royal, Manchester. *Programmes, 1861-1923*. 1861-1923. [Limited access. Incomplete. (Another *very* incomplete collection shelved Th792.094273 Ma 132/a.)]
Th792.094273 Ma132

[252] Theatre Royal, Manchester. *Playbill and Handbill: Aladdin and the Wonderful Lamp, 16th March, 1866.* 1866. [Printed on mauve silk, with black velvet border]
Th792.094273 Ma106

[253] Theatre Royal, Manchester. *The Church and the Stage: [a service at the Manchester Theatre Royal].* c.1871. [Proof copy of a periodical article]
L310/4

[254] Theatre Royal, Manchester. *Tickets for Various Benefit Performances, 1874-1875.*
Th792.094273 Ma280

[255] Theatre Royal, Manchester, and Manchester Prince's Theatre. *Pantomimes: Illustrations of Scenes extracted from various periodicals, 1874-84.*
792.094273

[256] Theatre Royal, Manchester. *Programme of the Performance of Shakespeare's Comedy 'As You Like It', October 1st and 2nd, 1879. List of Committee Members. Held at the Theatre Royal, Manchester.* Manchester, 1879.
792 1879/1/A M/cr

[257] Theatre Royal, Manchester. *Letters and Telegram, 1893-1894, between the Sisters Levey, T. Ramsay, Manager of the Theatre Royal, and solicitors, about an injunction to restrain the Sisters Levey from appearing anywhere in Manchester except the Theatre Royal, 1893-94.*
MSTh792.094273 Ma17

[258] Theatre Royal, Manchester. *Postcards of the cast of Mr. Tree's Company in Charles Dickens' "Oliver Twist".* [n.d.]
Th792.094273 Ma26

TIVOLI THEATRE OF VARIETIES

[259] Tivoli Theatre of Varieties, Manchester. *Programmes, 1883-1916.* Manchester, 1883-1916.
Th792.094273 Ma147

UNIVERSITY THEATRE

[260] 69 Theatre Company. *Past 69 Theatre Company productions.* 1976. [Photocopy of typescript. Includes productions at the University Theatre, Manchester, September 1968-1972, Royal Exchange, Manchester, May 1973- January 1975, touring Greater Manchester, October 1974-December 1975, and Edinburgh Festival, 1968.]
Th792.094273 Ma206

[261] Manchester University Theatre. *Playbills and Handbills, 1965-.* 1965-. [Limited access. Incomplete]
Th792.094273 Ma184

[262] Manchester University Theatre. *Productions Lists, 1965-.* 1965-. [Typescript]
ThF792.094273 Ma270

[263] Manchester University Theatre. *Programmes and Leaflets, 1965-.* 1965-. [Limited access. Incomplete]
Th792.094273 Ma183

WYTHENSHAWE FORUM THEATRE

[264] Wythenshawe Forum Theatre. *Chronological List of Performances. September 1971-.* 1971-. [See also Library Theatre for programmes, etc.]
Th792.094273 Wy1

Victor Rae as Ivanhoe.

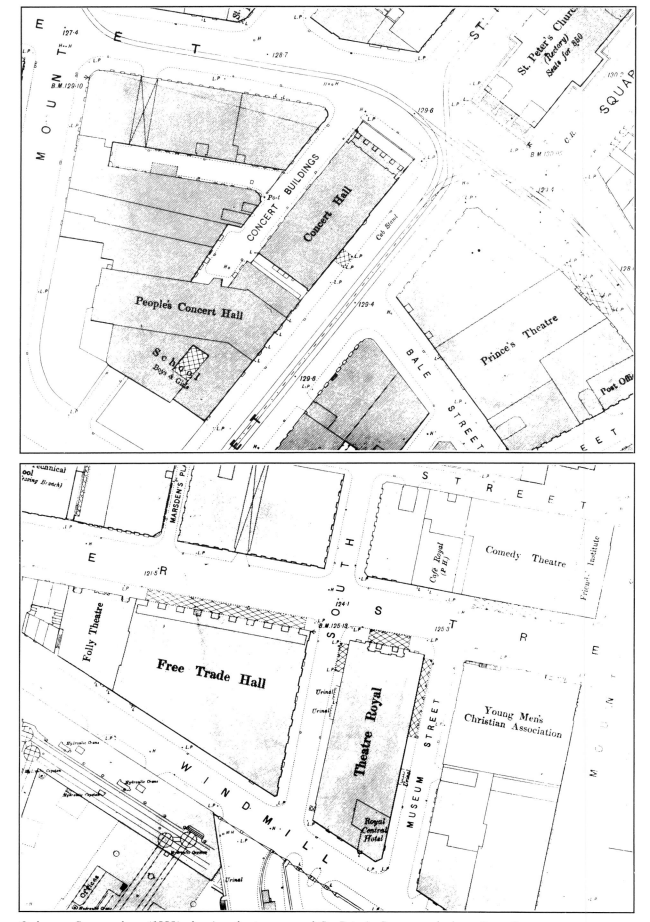

Ordnance Survey plans (1889) showing theatres around St. Peter's Square and along Peter Street.

III. LOCAL SURVEYS

[265] Adams, Arthur. *Ye Calverte Dramatick Societie's Horne Booke; or, ye Histrionick ABC.* Manchester: E. Hulton & Co., 1889.
Th792.094273 Ad1

[266] Agate, James. *Alarums and Excursions.* London: Grant Richards, 1922.
792 A31

[267] "A Lady Amateur Actress". *The Stage and Christianity Reconciled: the simple story of the real troubles and experience of an inquirer after truth; by a lady amateur actress of Manchester.* 1866.
L310/2

[268] Arnold, William Thomas, et al. *The Manchester Stage, 1880-1900: criticisms reprinted from the "Manchester Guardian".* Westminster: Archibald Constable & Co., 1900. [Oliver Elton, Allan Monkhouse and C. E. Montague also contributed.]
Th792.094273 Ar1

[269] Ashton, Mark. "Drama is Their Holiday Fare". *Lancashire Life* 5 (September 1957) 35, 37. [Summer school at Alston Hall College of Further Education organized by the Community Council of Lancashire.]
942.72 L330

[270] Axon, W.E.A. "The Cost of Theatrical Amusements". *Transactions of Manchester Statistical Society* (1881-2 Session) 177-87.
310.6 M1

[271] Battye, Thomas. *A Letter from Mr. B. to Miss F.* [In *Manchester Theatre Tracts.* A proposal of marriage.] Manchester: J. Leigh (printer), 1814.
L273/4

[272] Beverly, William. *The Beverly Administration; or, A Brief Sketch of the Manchester Stage.* Manchester: I. S. Gregson, 1828.
Th792 B9

[273] Bleackley, Edward Overall. *On Effective Reading: a paper.* Manchester, 1881. [On the value of elocution and recitation, with reminiscences of public readings by actors in Manchester.]
792.0942733 L522/8

[274] Brewer, Beth. "Theatre Workshop. Joan Littlewood sees a dream come true". *Lancashire Life,* 1 (1949) 235-6.
F942.72 L330

[275] Brighouse, Harold. "The Manchester Drama". *Papers of the Manchester Literary Club,* 43 (1917) 75-90.
806 M17

[276] Broadbent, R. J. *Annals of the Manchester Stage, 1735-1845.* Manchester, [n.d.] 3 vols. [Author's original typescript copy. Microfilm copy made by MPL in order to preserve the original (ThQ792.4273 B6). A typescript copy of the original may be available on prior written application at (ThF792.4273 B8). Also typed indexes to contents: v. 1. Plays; v. 1. Actors; v. 2 Plays; v. 2. Actors; v. 3. Compiled by the Society for Theatre Research, North West Group.
792.0942733 MF 125-126

[277] Broadbent, R. J. *Notable Events in Manchester Theatricals, 1735-1859; First Performances in Manchester at the Theatre Royal, 1776-1858; First Appearances at the Manchester Theatre Royal, 1774-1857.* [n.d.] [Typescript]
MSQ792.4273 B7

[278] Butterworth, Walter. *French Plays in Manchester.* Manchester, 1924. [Reprinted from *The Manchester Quarterly* 50 (1924) 215-24]
Th792.4273 B1

[279] Callender, E. Romaine. *Dr. Thomson on the Stage: A Reply.* Manchester: Heywood, 187-.
175.2 C12

[280] Charlton, H. B. "Manchester and the Drama" in W. H. Brindley (ed.), *The Soul of Manchester.* Manchester: Manchester University Press, 1929.
942.738 B63

[281] Cohen, Gerda. *Northern Footlights.* 1980. [Visits to Theatres in Manchester and Bolton.]
Q792 Co53

[282] Colley, David Isherwood. *A History of Repertory Theatre in Manchester, with particular reference to the Manchester Library Theatre.* Manchester, 1956. [Typescript]
Th792.094273 Co1

[283] Colley, David Isherwood. *The Modern Theatre.* Manchester, 1958. [Abridged from an address given to the Manchester Literary and Philosophical Society, 9th October 1958.]
ThF792.0942 Co17

[284] Community Council of Lancashire. County Drama Committee. *Drama in Lancashire.* Manchester, 1961.
792.094272 Co1

[285] Corlette, Charles Mayne. *The Universal Theatrical Stage Guide by Chas M. Corlette, theatrical agent, etc. 2 Snowden Street, Gaylor Street, Manchester.* Manchester, 1896. (1st ed.)

[286] Courtneidge, Robert. "The Amusements of Manchester" in C.W. Sutton (ed.), *Manchester of Today. Handbook and Guide to Manchester.* Manchester: Sherratt and Hughes, 1907 pp.199-203.

[287] D.A.L.T.A. (Dramatic and Lyric Theatres Association). *Dalta in the North West.* c.1970. [New functions as a department of the Arts Council solely concerned with the promotion of touring in regional centres.]
792.0942 Da1

[288] Darbyshire, Alfred. *Address delivered at the Arts Club, Manchester, April 22nd, 1893, by Alfred Darbyshire, F.S.A.* Manchester: Guardian Printing Works, 1894. [Part of a series entitled *Stage Representation of Shakespeare.* Darbyshire refers to Calvert's Shakespearean revivals at the Prince's Theatre.]
822.33 G3

[289] Darbyshire, Alfred. *Theatre Exits. A Paper by Alfred Darbyshire, architect...With a description and plan of Sir Henry Irving's "safety theatre".* Issued at the offices of the British Fire Prevention Committee: Charles & Edwin Layton, 1898. [*Publications of the British Fire Prevention Committee*, No. 4, ed. by Edwin O. Sachs. Bound in *Publications of the British Fire Prevention Committee*, Vol. I, 1898.]
704 Da1/3

[290] Dryden, Leo. *Song-Playlets and Popular Songs. G.D. Wheeler.* Manchester: Exchange Printing & Stationery Co., 19–. [Limited access]
Th792.094273 Dr096

[291] Edward, James. "Pantomime through a looking glass". *Lancashire Life* 5 (1957) 30-1.
F942.72 L330

[292] Ervine, St. John [Greer]. *The Repertory Theatres.* 1937. [A series of articles extracted from the Observer, April-August, 1937. Also two articles on the "Playhouse", Liverpool from the same paper, 8th & 15th December, 1935.]
792.0942 Er1

[293] Evans, John. "Reminiscences of the Stage in Manchester". *Papers of the Manchester Literary Club* 3 (1877) 193-5; 4 (1878) 227-31; 5 (1879) 246-8; 6 (1880) 290-4; 7 (1881) 350-3.
806 M17

[294] Fishwick, Henry (ed.) *Shakespearian Addresses delivered at the Arts Club, Manchester, 1886-1912.* London: Sherratt & Hughes, 1912.
822.33 G195

[295] Fitups of Manchester. *Everything for the Modern Stage,* c.1930.
792.025 Fi1

[296] Foulkes, Richard. *Charles Calvert's Henry V.* Cambridge: Cambridge University Press, 1989. [Reprinted from *Shakespeare Survey: An Annual Survey of Shakespeare Studies and Production,* Volume 41, p.23-34.]
Th792.094273 Fo1

[297] Fraser, James (Bishop of Manchester). *The Church and the Stage.* 1877. [Taken from *Victoria Magazine.* Bishop Fraser gave his sermon at the Theatre Royal, Manchester.]
L310/4

[298] Garrett, A. E. "The new amateur movement in Manchester". *English Review* 34 (April 1922) 348-54.
052 E20

[299] Granada TV Network. *Granada's Manchester Plays. Television adaptations of the six plays recalling the Horniman Period at the Gaiety Theatre, Manchester.* Manchester: Manchester University Press, 1962.

[300] Griffiths, Sian, and Anne Mayer, eds. *A Touring Company Guide to Greater Manchester and the North West.* Manchester, 1978. [New, revised ed. by Diane Bown.]
F792.09427 Gr1

[301] Guttenberg, Percy. *Picture Postcards of Actors and Actresses, taken in Manchester c.1900-1920.* 1900-20. [Limited access]
Th792.094273 Gu1

[302] Harland, John. "The older theatres and the drama in Manchester" *Manchester Collectanea,* Vol II pp.55-66 in *Chetham Society* Vol LXXII (1867)
942.7 C15

[303] Haworth, G. A., ed. *A Year in the Theatre, Greater Manchester 1993.* Manchester: Broadfield Publishing, 1993.
Th792.094273 Ye974

[304] Hayes, Susan. *Manchester's Lost Theatres.* 1977. [Typescript]
ThF792.094273 Ha2

[305] Hindsman, Bertha. "The Children's Theatre in Ancoats, 1922-47" *Social Welfare* 6 (1945-7) 302-4.
360 S1

[306] Hodgkinson, J. L., and Rex Pogson. *The Early Manchester Theatre*. London: Anthony Blond for the Society for Theatre Research, 1960. [Includes photographs used to illustrate the published works.]
ThF792.094273 Ho3; Th792.094273 Ho1

[307] Holland, Bertram H. *Beginners on Stage: the Story of the Stretford Children's Theatre*. London: Faber & Faber, 1968.
Th792.094273 Ho7

[308] Holt, Edgar. *Entertainments*. 13 vols. Manchester, 1924-28. [A handwritten account of theatre and cinema entertainment, mainly in Manchester.]
Th792.094273 Ho13

[309] Horrocks, Sidney. "The Manchester Theatre. Sources for Research in the Manchester Reference Library" *Manchester Review* 6 (1951) Winter 161-4, 200.
017.442 M62

[310] Horrocks, Sidney. "Materials for Theatre Research in the Manchester Reference Library". *Transactions of the North West Group Society for Theatre Research* I (1951) 4-7.
Th792.09427 S1

[311] Hughes, Chas. (ed.) *A Souvenir of the performance of Browning's tragedy, "A Blot in the 'Scutcheon", Manchester, March 27, 1893*. Manchester: Richard Gill (printer), 1893.

[312] Hulme, W. Arnold. "Early Manchester Theatres" *Transactions of the North West Group, Society for Theatre Research* I (1951) 7-8.
Th792.09427 S1

[313] Independent Theatre. Manchester Committee. *Shakespeare's King Richard II by Mr. Louis Calvert's Company: Programme*. 1895.
Th792.094273 In1

[314] Knowlson, Joyce, ed. *Chronological List of Performances at Manchester Theatres*.

Vol.1: Palace Theatre, May 1891-December 1963.

Vol.2: Hippodrome, Oxford Street, Boxing Day 1904-February 1935; Ardwick Empire, August 1904-October 1930; Ardwick Hippodrome, April 1935-December 1938. Tivoli, January 1901-August 1921.

Vol.3: Articles and pictures in "Manchester Programme", August 1897-January 1932; Stock repertory companies on Broadhead Circuit, Midland Hotel Theatre, September 1904-July 1920; Comedy/Gaiety Theatre, July 1897-April 1908; New Devonshire Theatre, Higher Broughton, December 1913-July

1914; Rusholme Electric Theatre (Repertory), January 1912-March 1926; Grand Theatre, January 1901-June 1915; Rusholme Pavilion (Leslie's), April 1906-August 1926; Chorlton Pavilion, July 1904-December 1908; Regent Theatre, Salford, August 1897-May 1907; Salford Palace, January 1920-March 1924; Victoria Theatre, Salford, January 1901-June 1918; Prince of Wales Theatre, Salford, February 1898-September 1905; Salford Hippodrome, July 1904-March 1934.

Vol.4: Local Manchester Actors and Actresses: Queen's Park Hippodrome, July 1904-May 1930; Hulme Hippodrome, July 1904-June 1933; Grand Junction Theatre, Hulme, October 1901-October 1920; Crown Theatre (formerly Lyceum), Eccles, March 1899-March 1932.

Vol.5: Osborne Theatre, August 1897-November 1932; Metropole Theatre, June 1898-March 1934; King's Theatre, November 1905-May 1933; Bury Hippodrome, January 1925-April 1929; Empire Hippodrome, Ashton-under-Lyne, January 1925-April 1929; Preston Hippodrome, June 1927-October 1928. 1973. [Manuscript]
ThF792.094273 Kn1

[315] Knowlson, Joyce, ed. *List of Theatres and Music Halls Taken from the "Era" Almanack, 1868-1910*. c.1974. [Theatres and music halls in Lancashire and Cheshire. Includes Manchester music halls. Manuscript]
Th792.094272 Kn1

[316] Knowlson, Joyce. *Red Plush and Gilt: The Heyday of Manchester Theatre during the Victorian and Edwardian Periods*. Manchester: The Author, 1985.
ThQ792.094273 Kn2

[317] Küttner, Karl Gottlob. *Schauspiel (At the Play)* Tr. by Peter W. Taylor, from the German. 1954. [Typescript]
F792.0942 K3

[318] Leach, Elizabeth. "The Manchester Theatre: Resources of the Arts Library". [Reprinted from *Manchester Review* 10 (Autumn 1965) 217-25.]
ThF792.094273 Le1; 017.442 M62

[319] Leach, Elizabeth. "Playbills and programmes". [Reprinted from *Manchester Review* 11 (Spring-Summer 1966) 7-22.]
ThF792.094273 Le2; 016.442 M62

[320] Lingard, T. W. A. *Manchester Theatres: Manuscript Articles, Reminiscences and Correspondence*. 192-. [Manuscript]
MSF792.094273 Li1

[321] *A Little Amusement for the Gentlemen of Monmouth-Street, Rosemary-Lane, and the Neighbourhood; vulgarly called Cannon-st. and McDonald's lane. With observations on clerical, military, mercantile, and theatrical characters.* Manchester: R. & W. Dean & Co., 1804.

[322] MacColl, Ewan. "Theatre of Action, Manchester" in Raphael Samuel, Ewan MacColl and Stuart Cosgrove (eds.), *Theatres of the Left 1880-1935. Workers' Theatre Movements in Britain and America.* London: Routledge & Kegan Paul, 1985.

[323] McGill, Hilda Mary. *A Playgoer of the Century.* 1975. [Reminiscences of a Manchester Playgoer. Includes some information on cinema. Typescript.]
ThMS792.094273 Ma285

[324] Manchester City Art Galleries. *International Theatre Exhibition [held from] October 5-November 18, 1922.* Manchester: Manchester City Art Gallery, 1922. [Catalogue]
792.074 Ma1

[325] Manchester Critic. *Manchester Theatres – Past and Present; by Apemantus.* 1875. [A series of ten press clippings]
B.R.FF792.094273 Ma283

[326] Manchester Evening News. *The Good Old Days: A Nostalgic Look at the Golden Years of the Theatre in Edwardian Manchester and the Boom Years of the Super Cinema.* Manchester Evening News special edition, 19th June 1976.
ThF792.094273 Ma250

[327] A Manchester Layman (pseud. of A. Gill) *The Theatre: its Character and Tendency: being a lecture delivered in the Free Library, Regent Road, Salford, February 22nd, 1877 . . . in reference to the recent utterances of the Bishop of Manchester on theatrical performances.* Manchester: John Heywood; Salford: Thomas Walker; London: Elliot Stock, 1877.

[328] Manchester Public Libraries. Archives Department. *References to Theatres, mainly in Manchester.* 19-. [Typescript]
F792.094273 Ma72

[329] Manchester Public Libraries. *Local Studies Print Collection: Theatres and Music Halls.*

[Includes prints of the following theatres:

Abbey Theatre, Dublin; Alexandra Music Hall, Peter Street; Alhambra Theatre, Openshaw; Ardwick Empire, Ardwick Green; Bridgewater Music Hall, Higher Cambridge Street; Canterbury Music Hall, Salford; Circus Theatre, Hulme; Coloseum Music Hall, Bridge Street; Concert Hall, Peter Street;

Crooked Billet Concert Room, Chapel Street, Salford; Dog and Partridge Music Hall, Oldham Road; Empress Electric Theatre, Oldham Road; Electric Theatre, Oldham; Folly Theatre of Varieties, Peter Street; Gaiety Theatre, Peter Street; Garrick Theatre, Altrincham; Gentlemen's Concert Hall, Peter Street; Grand Junction Theatre, Hulme; Grand Theatre of Varieties, Peter Street; Harte's Theatre, Bradford; Hulme Hippodrome; Junction Theatre; King's Theatre, Longsight; Manchester Hippodrome, Oxford Street; Manchester University Theatre; Marsden Street Theatre; The Melodrama Audience; Metropole Theatre, Higher Openshaw; Midland Theatre; New Manchester Hippodrome, Ardwick Green; New Pavilion, Spring Gardens; Olympia Theatre; Olympic Theatre, Stevenson Square; Opera House, Quay Street; Osborne Theatre, Oldham Road; Palace Theatre; Paramount Theatre, Oxford Street; People's Theatre, Lower Mosley Street; Prince's Theatre, Oxford Street; A Pub Theatre, Cambridge Street; Queen's Park Hippodrome, Harpurhey; Queen's Theatre, Bridge Street; Queen's Theatre, Spring Gardens; Regent Hotel Music Hall, Deansgate; Rising Sun Music Hall, Swan Street; Rowland Hill Concert Room, Manchester; Royal Exchange Theatre; Rusholme Theatre; St. James's Theatre, Oxford Street; Stand Grammar School Drama Society; Tatler Theatre site; Theatre Royal, Bury; Theatres Royal, Manchester; Tivoli Theatre, Peter Street.

[330] Manchester Theatre. *Newspaper Clippings: Theatrical Criticism, Manchester and District, 1903-1928.* 2 vols. 1903-28.
ThQ792.094273 Ne1

[331] *Manchester Theatres: Copies of Plans deposited in the City Architect's Department.* [n.d.] [Contents: 1. New Theatre (Opera House). 2. Palace Theatre. 3. Gaiety & Prince's Theatres. 4. Manchester Hippodrome, Oxford Street; Ardwick Empire (New Manchester Hippodrome, Ardwick Green). 5. Queen's Park Hippodrome; Grand Junction Theatre & Hulme Hippodrome. 6. King's Theatre (Opera House, Longsight); Metropole Theatre; Osborne Theatre (Olympia, Oldham Road). Photocopies in portfolios]
ThFF725.82 Ma7

[332] Manchester Theatres. *Newspaper Clippings: Manchester Theatres, 17–.*

Note: This collection of newspaper cuttings forms a major part of the Theatre Collection. It comprises some 50 box files of cuttings from north-west newspapers and publications. The cuttings include coverage of Manchester theatres, theatre companies, societies, reviews of performances, reminiscences and personal profiles. A summary is given below.

Contents: (number of boxes per subject in brackets): A-Z Manchester Theatres (8); Civic Theatre (1); Contact Theatre (2); Gaiety Theatre (1); Green Room (1); Manchester Cinemas A-Z (3); Nia Centre (1); Northern Ballet Dance Theatre (1); Opera House (7); Palace Theatre (7); Prince's Theatre (1); Royal Exchange Theatre (including Corn Exchange and Youth Theatres) (4); Rusholme (Manchester Repertory) Theatre (1); 69 Theatre Company (1); Stables Theatre (1); Theatres Royal (1); Theatre for Young People and Theatre in Education (1); University Theatre (including Stephen Joseph and Brickhouse Studios) (1); General History, 1729- (1); Amateur Dramatic Societies (2); Theatres in general (1).
Th792.094273 Ne6

[333] Manchester Theatres. *Newspaper cuttings of articles on Manchester theatres*, 19–.
Th792.094273 Ma44

[334] Manchester Theatres. *Scrapbook of miscellaneous newspaper cuttings related to Manchester theatres, 1929-1953.* 2 vols. 1929-53.
ThF792.094273 Sc100

[335] Manchester Theatres. *Newspaper Cuttings: Manchester Theatre, 1907-1913.* [Reviews; biographical and general articles, etc. Includes some articles on London theatre, 1907-13.
Th792.094273 Ne5

[336] Mayer, David. "The World on Fire . . . Pyrodramas at Belle Vue Gardens, Manchester, c.1850-1950." in John M. Mackenzie (ed.), *Popular Imperialism and the Military 1850-1950.* Manchester: Manchester University Press, 1992.
325.32 Im2

[337] Mellor, G.J. *The Northern Music Hall. A Century of Popular Entertainment.* Newcastle upon Tyne: Frank Graham, 1970.

[338] Montague, Charles Edward. *Dramatic Values.* London: Methuen, 1911.
792 M39

[339] North West Arts Association. Theatre Enquiry Committee. *A New Stage. Theatre in the Greater Manchester Area. Report of the Theatre Enquiry Committee of the North West Arts Association.* Manchester: North West Arts Association, 1972.
Q792.09427 No4

[340] Parkin, Wilf. *Salford Theatres and Music Halls, 1880-1980.* Salford: The Author, 1980. (3rd ed.)
ThQ792.094273 Pa3

[341] Pease, David. *A Handbook and Directory of Arts in the North West.* Manchester: North West Arts Association, 1972.

[342] "Play-bill relating to the burning of the Theatre Royal, Manchester" *Local Gleanings*, 1 (1875-6) No.476.
942.7 L2

[343] Pogson, Rex. "The Pantomime Tradition" *Manchester Review* (1955)
016.442 M62

[344] Procter, Richard Wright. *Manchester in Holiday Dress.* Manchester: Abel Heywood & Son, 1866. [A history of theatrical and other forms of public entertainment.]
Th792.094273 P1

[345] Procter, Richard Wright. *Our Turf, Our Stage and Our Ring.* Manchester: Abel Heywood & Son, 1862.
798 P1

[346] Select Committee on Theatrical Licenses and Regulations. *Report: with Proceedings, Minutes of evidence and appendix.* 1866. Parliamentary Papers 1866 (373) XVI. [Includes evidence relating to Manchester theatres.]
[792.0942733] Sess Papers, 1866

[347] Smith, R. *The "Christian World" and the Theatre.* Manchester: John Heywood, 1879.
L310/3

[348] Society for Theatre Research. North West Group. *Two Hundred Years of Theatre in Manchester, in the Exhibition Hall, Central Library, October 6th to 25th, 1952.* Manchester: The Society, 1952. [Contents: Hulme, W. A.; Notes on some of the more important theatres. Crogan, Antony; A list of theatres and music halls.]
792.094273 S1

[349] Society for Theatre Research. North West Group, and Rex Pogson. *The Panto Story: [Handbook to] an Exhibition of Playbills, Model Theatres, Designs, Prints and Photographs in the Central Library, Manchester, 9th January-4th February, 1956.* Manchester: Richard Bates (printer) for the Society for Theatre Research, 1956.
Th792.3 S1

[350] Southam, Thomas. *The Theatre.* Eccles: The Author, 1876.
L310/6

[351] Spafford, Ernest. *Ernest Spafford, Concert Agent, Hooley Hill, Manchester. Catalogue of Artistes.* Manchester: F. Smith (printer), [n.d.]
Th791.094273 Sp295

[352] *The Theatre. Its Injurious Influence on the Community and the consequent obligations of those who make a Serious Profession of the Gospel. Stated and Illustrated.* Edinburgh: printed for Ogle, Allardice and Thomson, 1820.
L310/1

[353] Theatrical Children Licences Committee. *Report.* 1919. (Cmd. 484) (Board of Education). Chairman: F. H. Oates.]
PARL F331.3 E1

[354] Waters, Chris. "Manchester Morality and London Capital: the Battle over the Palace of Varieties" in Peter Bailey (ed.), *Music Hall. The Business of Pleasure.* Milton Keynes: Open University Press, 1986.

[355] Watters, Eugene, and Matthew Murtagh. *Infinite Variety: Dan Lowrey's Music Hall, 1879-97.* 1975.
792.7 Wa1

[356] S. B. Watts & Co. Ltd. *Looking the Part. [S. B. Watts and Co., Ltd., the Manchester based theatrical costumiers].* 1981. [Photocopied extract from the British Theatre Institute] 38 of <u>Theatre Newsletter</u>.
Th792.026 Lo1

[357] Wewiora, George E. "Manchester Music-Hall Audiences in the 1880s". *Manchester Review* 12 (1973) 124-8.
017.442 M62

[358] Williamson, Robert J. R. *The Manchester Theatre.* <u>Society for Theatre Research. Lecture Reports</u>, 1966.
Th792.094273 Wi4

[359] Winder, Eileen. *The Public Library and the Theatre in Manchester.* Manchester, 1979. [Typescript]
ThF027.442733 Wi1

[360] Wood, F. T. "Notes on English Provincial Playhouse in the Eighteenth Century". *Notes and Queries* 160 (January-June 1931) 147-50, 165-9, 183-7. [Includes Liverpool and Manchester.]
792.0942

[361] Yates, Frederick. *Musical, Concert and Variety Artistes' Agency. List of Artistes.* Failsworth, Manchester: Fielding (printer), [n.d.]
Th791.094273 Ya1

[362] *Young People's Theatre, Committee of Enquiry, 1972-1973. Half-Price? The Provision of Professional Theatre for Young People in the North West: the Report to the North West Arts Association.* 1974. [Chair: Cora Williams.]
Q792.09427 Yo1

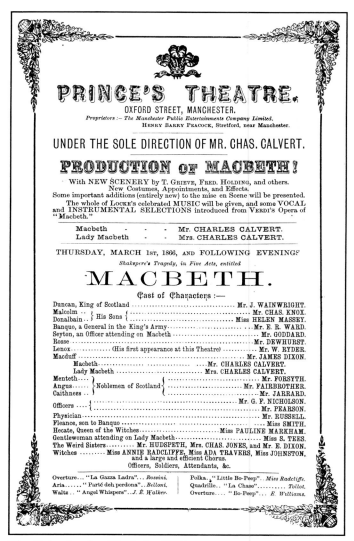

The Calverts play Macbeth, 1866.

IV. BIOGRAPHICAL MATERIAL

[363] Agate, James. *Ego. The Autobiography of James Agate.* London: Hamilton, 1935.
928.28 A47

[364] Agate, James. *Ego 2, being more of the Autobiography.* London: Gollancz, 1936.
928.28 A48

[365] Agate, James. *Ego 3, being still more of the Autobiography.* London: Harrap, 1940.
928.28 A49

[366] Agate, James. *Ego 4, yet more of the Autobiography.* London: Harrap, 1940.
928.28 A50

[367] Agate, James. *Ego 5, again more of the Autobiography.* London: Harrap, 1942.
928.28 A51

[368] Agate, James. *Ego 6, once more the Autobiography.* London: Harrap, 1944.
928.28 A46

[369] Agate, James. *Ego 7, even more of the Autobiography.* London: Harrap, 1945.
928.28 A45

[370] Agate, James. *Ego 8, continuing the Autobiography.* London: Harrap, 1946.
928.28 A60

[371] Agate, James. *Ego 9, concluding the Autobiography.* London: Harrap, 1948.
928.28 A61

[372] Agate, James. *These Were Actors. Extracts from a Newspaper Cuttings Book 1811-1833. Selected and Annotated by James Agate.* London: Hutchinson, 1943. [Contains criticisms of English actors and actresses, particularly Edmund Kean.]
792.42 A14

[373] Bendle, Alan, and Joyce Knowlson. *Curtain Call: Personal Reminiscences by Alan Bendle and Historical Detail by Joyce Knowlson, on the Manchester Theatre [1900-c.1959].* 196-. [Author's carbon typescript, copyright reserved. Limited access]
Th792.094273 Be1

[374] Brighouse, Harold. *Hobson's Choice, a Three-Act Comedy. With an Introduction by B. Iden Payne.* London: Constable, 1916.
822.9 B32

[375] Brighouse, Harold. *What I Have Had. Chapters in Autobiography.* London: Harrap, 1953.

[376] Bunnage, Avis, and Harry H. Corbett. *Photographs, Theatre Programmes, Newspaper Clippings, etc., relating to Avis Bunnage and Harry H. Corbett, 1949-1990.* 1949-90. [Includes performances in Manchester. Limited access]
ThF792.094273 Bu227

[377] Calvert, Adelaide Helen [Mrs Charles Calvert]. *Sixty-Eight Years on the Stage.* London: Mills & Boon, 1911. [Biddles, Adelaide]
Th792.094273 Ca9

[378] Calvert, Charles Alexander. *Biographical Material.* [n.d.] [Calvert (1828-79) was principally connected with the Theatre Royal and the Prince's Theatre, and famed for his Shakespearean revivals.]
Th792.094273 Ca2

[379] Casson, John. *Lewis and Sybil. A Memoir.* London: Collins, 1972.
792.0942 Ca1

[380] Charles, Thomas W., ed. *Memorials of Charles Calvert's productions of Shakespeare and the poetic drama.* London: William Aubert, 1875.
Th792.0942 Ch1

[381] Cogdill, Jack. *Contents of Letters to Miss Horniman.* 1977. [Typescript index]
Th792.094273 Ho10

[382] Courtneidge, Cicely. *Cicely.* London: Hutchinson, 1953.
927.92 Co4

[383] Courtneidge, Robert. *"I Was an Actor Once".* London, Hutchinson, 1930.
927.92 C65

[384] Darbyshire, Alfred. *An Architect's Experiences: Professional, Artistic, and Theatrical. By Alfred Darbyshire, F.S.A., F.I.B.A.* Manchester: J. E. Cornish, 1897. [Another copy at **BR927.92 D1/a** with the author's presentation inscription to Anna Gertrude Darbyshire. Also, author's copy with extra illustrations at **BR927.2 D1/b** (2 vols) bound by Palmer, Howe & Co.]
927.2 D1

[385] Darbyshire, Alfred. *The Art of the Victorian Stage: Notes and Recollections.* Manchester: Sherratt & Hughes, 1907.
Th792.0942 Da1

[386] Dean, Basil. *The Basil Dean Collection in the John Rylands Library of the University of Manchester.* c.1989. 2 of Theatre History Series. [99 Microfiche]
MFE792.094273 De499

[387] Dean, Basil. *Seven Ages. An Autobiography, 1888-1927*. London: Hutchinson, 1970.
927.92 De4

[388] Dean, Basil. *Mind's Eye. An Autobiography, 1927-1972*. London: Hutchinson, 1973.
927.92 De4

[389] Devlin, Diana. *A Speaking Part. Lewis Casson and the Theatre of His Time*. London: Hodder & Stoughton, 1982.
792.028 Ca2

[390] Easby, John. *Random Scenes from the life of a green-coated schoolboy; his trials on the stage, the press, the platform, and the pulpit. Written, from memory, by himself*. Manchester: Abel Heywood, 1851. [Attributed to the journalist, John Easby.]
920.5 E6

[391] Foulkes, Richard. *The Calverts: Actors of Some Importance*. London: Society for Theatre Research, 1992.
Th792.028 Ca484

[392] Gooddie, Sheila. *Annie Horniman: a Pioneer in the Theatre*. London: Methuen, 1990.
792.984273 Ho481

[393] Greenwich Theatre. *A Festival for Miss Horniman, April-July 1978: Plays, Films, Talks, Exhibition*. London: Greenwich Theatre Festival, 1978.
Th792.094273 Ho22

[394] Holbrook, Ann Catherine. *Memoirs of an Actress, comprising a faithful narrative of her theatrical career from 1798 to the present period, giving a lively picture of the stage in general, and interspersed with a variety of anecdotes, humourous and pathetic. By Ann Catherine Holbrook, late of the new Theatre Royal, Manchester*. Manchester: J. Harrop at the Mercury Office, 1807.

[395] Horniman, Annie Elizabeth Fredericka. *The Annie Horniman Collection in the John Rylands University Library of Manchester*. 1989. 1 of Theatre History Series. [27 volumes on 77 fiche]
MFE 792.094273 Ho500

[396] Horniman, Annie Elizabeth Fredericka. *The Horniman Festival: a Scrapbook of Newspaper Cuttings commemorating the fiftieth anniversary of the Repertory Theatre Movement and of the founding of the Gaiety Theatre, Manchester by Miss A.E.F. Horniman*. 1958.
Th792.094273 H1

[397] Horniman, Annie Elizabeth Fredericka. *Letters to Tom Bass, 1919-1936*. [Manuscripts. Includes picture postcards and photographs.]
MSF927.92 Ho1

[398] Horniman, Annie Elizabeth Fredericka. *Miscellaneous Collection of Newspaper Clippings and Photographs, 1907-1978*. 1907-1978.
Th792.094273 Ho16

[399] Horniman, Annie Elizabeth Fredericka. *Miscel-laneous Collection of Photographs, Letters, etc.* [n.d.]
Th792.094273 Ho17

[400] Horniman, Annie Elizabeth Fredericka. *Programmes of Performances given by Miss Horniman's Company at Marple (1909) and at Ancoats, Manchester (1910)*. 1910.
ThQ792.094273 Ho23

[401] Horniman, Annie Elizabeth Fredericka. *"A Talk A bout the Drama." Manchester Statistical Society. Read 14th December, 1910*. Manchester: John Heywood Ltd., 1910.
Th792.094273 Ho9

[402] Horniman, Annie Elizabeth Fredericka. *A Testimonial to Miss Horniman Bearing Fifteen Signatories, with an Accompanying Article, 1910*.
ThFF792.094273 Ho18

[403] Horniman, Annie Elizabeth Fredericka. *Two colour photographs of Miss Horniman's Companion of Honour and her dragon brooch*. [n.d.]
ThFF792.094273 Ho19

[404] Houghton, Stanley. *Letter to a Mr. Whelan dated June 19 1912 which includes a reference to Annie Horniman of the Gaiety Theatre, Manchester*. 1912. [Manuscript]
Th792.094273 Ho14

[405] Irving, Sir Henry. *Henry Irving in all his Principal Characters, 1866-1890. Drawn by Fred Barnard from special sittings*. [Limited access. Supplement to *Black and White*, 23 May 1891.]
ThFF792.094273 Ir472

[406] Irving, Laurence. *Henry Irving: the Actor and His World*. London: Columbus Books, 1989.
927.92 I16

[407] Lind, Jenny. *Playbills and Reviews of the Jenny Lind Tours of Provincial Theatres, from August 1847-October 1848*. 1847-48.
ThFF792 Li5

[408] Liston, Harry. *Notes and Extracts, etc., relating to Harry Liston, Comedian and Owner of Liston's Bar in Manchester*. 1903-50. [Collected by Brian Tagg. Harry Liston's real name was John Greenhalgh, sometimes spelt Greenhough.]
Th792.7 Li1

[409] Lloyd-Lewis, Howard. *Howard Lloyd-Lewis: a Celebration [held at the] Forum Theatre, Wythenshawe, Sunday 15 March 1987*. Manchester: Library Theatre Co., 1987. [Limited access]
ThQ792.094273 Ll289

[410] Manchester Public Libraries. *Annie E. F. Horniman, 1860-1937: Catalogue of an Exhibition held at Manchester Central Library during September 1978*. c.1978. [Includes a set of photographs of the exhibition.]
Th792.094273 Ho15

[411] Manchester Public Libraries. Archives Department. *Catalogue of Mathews Theatrical Portraits*. 1833.
MS792.42 M41

[412] Manchester Public Libraries. Archives Department. *Letters of Mrs. Leo Grindon about theatre*. [n.d.]

[413] Manchester Public Libraries. Archives Department. *Letters to Alfred Brothers from actresses and playwrights*. [18–].
BRF091 B60

[414] Manchester Public Libraries. Archives Department. *Letters to Charles Swain, including some from actresses*. [18–].
MSF091 S24

[415] Manchester Theatres. *Autograph Letters by people connected with Manchester Theatres and their administration, 1906-*. 1906-.
ThF792.094273 Ma263

[416] Manchester Theatres. *Autographs of Stage Personalities playing in Manchester Theatres*. 1903-7. [Limited access]
Th792.094273 Au265

[417] Mander, Raymond, and Joe Mitchenson. *Tribute to Miss Horniman*. London: Greenwich Theatre, 1978.
Th792.094273 Ho21

[418] *The Misses Terry: notes on "Much Ado About Nothing"; by a Lady and a Gentleman*. Manchester, 1867. [in Vol.1 of Cuttings, etc. relating to the Manchester stage. Suggested by Kate and Ellen Terry's performance at the Prince's Theatre.]
792.4273 M26

[419] Monkhouse, A. N. *Dramatic Criticism*. Manchester: William Hough & Sons, 1908.

[420] Morley, Sheridan. *Sybil Thorndike: a Life in the Theatre*. London: Weidenfeld & Nicolson, 1977.
792.028 Th1

[421] Mortimer, Paul. "W. Stanley Houghton: An Introduction and a Bibliography" *Modern Drama* 28 (1985)

[422] Murray, Christopher. *Robert William Elliston, Manager: a Theatrical Biography*. London: Society for Theatre Research, 1975. [Contains references to Liverpool and Manchester]
792.0942 El4

[423] Neilson, Harold V. *Biographical material*. [n.d.] [Includes a partial typescript by H. M. Walbrook, entitled *Harold V. Neilson: an Appreciation and a Forecast*. Neilson was born Thomas Clegg in Manchester, on 8.1.1874, became an actor, director and manager in London and the provinces. He died on 18.2.1956 in Virginia Water. Contains correspondence, photographs, programmes and criticism.]
Th792.094273 Ne10

[424] Parry, Edward Abbott. *What the Judge Saw; being twenty-five years in Manchester by one who has done it*. London: John Murray, 1912. [Includes a chapter on the Manchester stage and Parry's plays.]
923.4 P14

[425] Payne, Ben Iden. *A Life in a Wooden O. Memoirs of the Theatre*. New Haven: Yale University Press, 1977.
Th792.0942 Pa1

[426] *Picture Postcards of Stage Personalities, 1900-1920*. 1900-20. [Limited access. 123 postcards, some autographed.]
Th792.094273 Pi118

[427] Pogson, Rex. *Miss Horniman and the Gaiety Theatre, Manchester*. London: Rockliff, 1952.
Th792.0942 H1

[428] Rae, Victor. *Press clippings, photographs, part-books etc.* 1904-57. [3 boxes of scripts, play books, correspondence and photographs. Victor Rae was the stage name of Stanley Arthur May, actor and manager, of Urmston.]
MSF927.92 Ra1

[429] Rowell, George. *The Merchant of Manchester*. Reprint from Gilbert and Sullivan Journal, Spring 1974, p.81-3. [Biography of Charles Calvert.]
Th792.094273 Ca8

[430] Russell, Billy. *Miscellaneous Letters 1951-2*.
ThF792.028 Ru1

[431] Sackville-West, Reginald R. *Theatres of Manchester: nostalgic recollections*. Manchester, [n.d.] [Typescript]
ThF792.094273 Sa1

[432] Shelton, George. *It's Smee*. London, 1928. [Theatrical reminiscences. The author played the part of "Smee" in *Peter Pan* at the Prince's Theatre.] **927.92 S57**

[433] Sladen-Smith, F. "Reminiscences of a Mancunian Playgoer." *Drama* 1, No.2 (1919) 41-4. **792.42 D20**

[434] Sprigge, Elizabeth. *Sybil Thorndike Casson. With a foreword by Dame Sybil*. London: Gollancz, 1971. **792.0942 Th7**

[435] Stocks, Mary Danvers [Baroness Stocks]. *Still More Commonplace: autobiography*. 1973. [Includes a chapter on Rusholme Repertory Theatre, and Unnamed Society.] **Th920.7 St40/a**

[436] *Theatre Roundabout, 1960-1970: 10 years – 1,000 performances*. A touring company of two performers, Sylvia Reed and William Fry. c.1970. **792 Th15**

[437] Thorndike, Russell. *Sybil Thorndike*. London: Rockliff, 1950. [1st ed. (1929) at **927.92 T44**. The 2nd edition has an additional *Epilogue*.] **927.92 T45**

[438] Trewin, J. C. *Sybil Thorndike*. London: Rockliff, 1955. (Theatre World Monographs series) [An illustrated study of Dame Sybil's work, with a list of appearances on stage and screen.] **792 T23**

[439] Wewiora, George E. *The Great Actor-Managers in Manchester, 1880-1910*. 1973. [Typescript of a talk given at the Manchester Library Theatre.] **ThF792.094273 We1**

[440] Wewiora, George E. "J. T. Haines in Manchester, 1828-29". *Theatre Notebook* 27 (Spring 1973) 89-94. **Th792.094273 Ha1**

[441] White, J. F. *An Appeal to the Public at Large, of the Town of Manchester, but chiefly addressed to the violent opposers of J. F. White, comedian: with many particular observations on the management of theatres, and the peculiar situation of performers in general*. Manchester: G. Bancks (printer), 1803.

Harold V. Neilson in A Fool's Paradise, 1904.

V. THEATRE GROUPS AND THEATRICAL SOCIETIES

[442] Atkinson, James Augustus. *Christmas Entertainments and Sketches for amateur performance at St John's School, Longsight.* 18–. [Typescript]
792.0942733 L550

[443] Dawson, Nita A. *One Hundred Years of Amateur Acting: [Manchester Athenaeum Dramatic Society Commemoration Centenary, May 1947].* Manchester: Jesse Broad & Co. Ltd. (printers), 1947.
Th792.094273 Ma52

[444] Goethe Institute, Manchester. *Dramatic Performances, etc.: Programmes, Handbills, etc.* Manchester: Goethe Institute, 1969-. [Limited access]
Th792.094273 Go1

[445] Manchester Amateur Dramatic Society. *Minute Book.* 1877-1892.
Th792.094273 Ma155

[446] Manchester Amateur Dramatic Society. *Programmes.* 1879-1912. [Includes some performances by other local amateur societies]
Th792.094273 Ma156

[447] Manchester Amateur Dramatic Society. *Programmes and Clippings.* 1880-1900. [Includes Altrincham and Bowdon A. D. S., Sale A.D. Club and various church societies]
Th792.094273 Ma158

[448] Manchester Amateur Dramatic Society. *Programmes, etc.* 2 vols. 1879-1910. [Includes photographs, leaflets, tickets and a pamphlet giving the history of the Society]
Th792.094273 Ma157

[449] Manchester Amateur Dramatic Society. *Annual Report 1883-84,-1900-01.* 1884-1901. [Incomplete]
Th792.094273 Ma159

[450] *Manchester and District Amateur Theatrical Performances: Handbills, Posters, etc.,* 196-.
Th792.094273 Ma141

[451] *Manchester and District Amateur Theatrical Performances: Programmes.* 1877-1966. [Contents include programmes for the following societies:

Altrincham and Bowdon A.D.S.; Burnage Hall: Burnage High School A.D.S.; Central High School A.D.S.; Chorlton Road Congregational Church Y.P.F. Players; Christie Cancer Hospital; Chronicle Cinderella Club; Crumpsall Garrick Society; Didsbury O.A.D.S.; Ellerslie; Fairfield Hall; Higher Broughton A.O.D.S.; Lancashire Catholic Players' Society; Loreto Convent Hall; Lower Mosley Street Adult Education Institute, Manchester; Manchester Grammar School; Manchester School of Art; Manchester Ship Canal O.A.D.S.; Manchester University Classical Society; Moseley Road School; Owens College Shakespeare Society; Prestwich Dramatic Society; Princess Road Board School; Queen's Hall; St. Chrystostom's Church; St. Luke's, Cheetham; Sale A.D.S.; South Manchester O.A.D.S.; Victoria O.A.D.S; Tootal Dramatic Society; Chronicle players; St. George's Abbey Hey A.O.D.S.; Charles Dickens A.O.D.S.; Kenmil Players; C.W.S. Balloon Street Players; St. John's Players (Moston); The Old Waconians Associations; Manchester Y.M.C.A. Dramatic Society; Provincial Players; E.M.A.D.S.]
Th792.094273 Ma140

[452] *Manchester and District Library Fellowship Dramatic Section. Minutes, cash book, etc.* 1929-1946. [Later merged with Manchester Public Libraries Staff Association Dramatic Society.]
Th792.094273 Ma160

[453] *Manchester and District Library Fellowship Dramatic Section. Programmes, Clippings, Photographs.* 1929-40.
Th792.094273 Ma161

[454] Manchester Athenaeum Dramatic Society. c.1800-1961. *Programmes of Manchester Dramatic Societies, Clubs, etc.* [Contents: Manchester Athenaeum, Independent Stage Society, Independent Theatre, Experimental Theatre Club, Green Room Theatre, Chorlton Repertory Theatre Club, Manchester Ballet Club, Heaton Park Open Air Theatre]
Th792.094273 Ma138

[455] Manchester Central High School for Boys. *Dramatic Productions; Miscellaneous Material.* 2 vols. Manchester, 1922-26. [Includes photographs, newspaper cuttings, programmes and pamphlets.]
792.0942 Ma29

[456] Manchester Jewish Amateur Operatic Society. *San Toy: [programme].* 7-10 & 12th March 1921 Gaiety Theatre, Manchester. Manchester: Manchester Jewish and Operatic Society, 1921.
792.6 Ma4

[457] Manchester Jewish Lads' Brigade and Club. *Bugles, Belles and Beat: a Review [programme].* 1964.
Q792.094273 Ma35

[458] Manchester Playgoers' Club. *"21": A Labour of Love.* Manchester: J. E. Mulligan, 1929. [Published to commemorate the club's 21st anniversary.]
ThQ792.094273 Ma69

[459] Manchester Playgoers' Club. *Annual Report and Balance Sheet.* 1914/15-1931 Manchester: Manchester Playgoers' Club, 1914-31.
Th792 M24

[460] Manchester Playgoers' Club. *Collection of Letters, 1914-1930, from various writers prominently connected with the theatre, relating to functions of the Manchester Playgoers' Club.* 1914-30. [Most of the signatures have been removed for facsimile reproduction in *A Labour of Love.* (792.4273 M21).]
ThQ792.094273 Ma56

[461] Manchester Playgoers' Club. *Minutes of Committees and Annual General Meetings, 1908-1927. With Annual Reports and Balance Sheets, 1916-1926.* 3 vols. 1908-27. [Includes some correspondence.]
MS792.094273 M1

[462] Manchester Playgoers' Club. *Provisional Scheme [for a proposed civic theatre] deposited with the Lord Mayor of Manchester, February 9th, 1928.* 1928. [Address (signed by the Officers and Committee of the Club) presented to the Lord Mayor. In art leather-work cover.]
MSQ792.4273 M2

[463] Manchester Playgoers' Club. *Scrapbook.* 1909-1912. [Includes newspaper cuttings, play-reading cards and dinner menus.]
ThF792.094273 Ma32

[464] Manchester Polytechnic Theatre Society. *Newsletters, Leaflets, etc.* Manchester, 1973-. [Limited access]
Th792.094273 Ma175

[465] Manchester Public Libraries. Archives Department. *The Withington Players Amateur Dramatic Society: a Calendar.* 1977. [Guide to the papers.]
F792.094273 Ma252

[466] Manchester Public Libraries. Theatre Collection. *Chronological List of Programmes in the Collection: the Unnamed Society, 1918-1950.* Manchester, 197-. [Typescript]
Th792.094273 Ma174

[467] Manchester University. *Dramatic Performances excluding those given at University Theatre: Leaflets etc.* Manchester, 196-. [Includes productions of the Manchester University Stage Society, Drama Group, Drama Club, Dept. of Education and others. Limited access. Incomplete.]
Th792.094273 Ma180

[468] North Manchester Amateur Operatic Society. *Programmes.* Manchester, 1967-.
Th792.094273 Ma79

[469] The Play Society, Manchester. *Prospectus, 1919-1920.* Manchester: The Society, 1919-20.
Th792.094273 Ma261

[470] Sale Amateur Dramatic Club. *List of Officers for Season 1890-91.* Manchester: George Falkner and Sons, [n.d.] [Also contains *A Record of Twenty-One Years' Performances. 1869-1890.*]
Q792 S10

[471] Savage Club. *The Savage Club in Manchester. Performance in aid of the fund for the relief of the unemployed operatives, [in the] Free Trade Hall, September 2nd 1862. Programme.* Manchester: William Chilton, 1862.
Th792.094273 Sa3

[472] Sladen-Smith, F. *The Amateur Producer's Handbook.* London: University of London Press, 1933.

[473] University of Manchester Institute of Science and Technology. *Theatrical Performances: Handbills, Leaflets, etc.* 197-. [Limited access. Incomplete]
Th792.094273 Ma187

[474] Unnamed Society, Manchester. *Programmes.* Manchester, 1918-50.
Th792.094273 Un1

[475] Unnamed Society, Manchester. *Prospectuses, Photographs, Leaflets, etc.* Manchester, 1919-31.
.094273 Un4

[476] Unnamed Society, Manchester. *The Unnamed Book.* Manchester: Sherratt & Hughes, 1924. [Contributions, literary and artistic, by members including F. Sladen-Smith; descriptive of the society's dramatic work.]
ThF792.094273 Ma27

[477] Unnamed Society, Manchester. *The Unnamed Society's 21st Birthday, 1915-1936.* Manchester, "1936. [Contains an article on the society by Neville Cardus.]
Th792.094273 Ma58

[478] Unnamed Society, Manchester. *Water-colour sketches by Karl Hagedorn* [19–].

[479] Workers Educational Association Dramatic Society. Manchester and Salford Branch. *The W.E.A.D.S. Magazine.* Vol. 3, no. 3, Jan-Feb 1926.
Th792.094273 Wo1

LATE TRAINS.

From VICTORIA STATION—

To BOLTON and intermediate Stations (except Dixon Fold) 9-30, 10-50
„ ECCLES only 10-45
„ WEASTE, ECCLES, and PATRICROFT......10-15, 11-15
„ MIDDLETON JUNCTION, WERNETH, and OLDHAM.....................................10-0, 11-15
„ CASTLETON and ROCHDALE 10-15, 11-10
„ NEWTON BRIDGE and WIGAN................. 10-45
„ MILES PLATTING, CLAYTON BRIDGE, DROYLSDEN, ASHTON, & STALYBRIDGE 9-40, 11- 5
„ ASHTON and STALYBRIDGE, Thursdays and Saturdays only 10-35
„ HEYWOOD and BURY.....................9-25, 11-10

From CENTRAL STATION—

To ALTRINCHAM, KNUTSFORD, and NORTHWICH.. 10-40
„ URMSTON, FLIXTON, IRLAM, WARRINGTON, FARNWORTH, GARSTON, and LIVERPOOL 11- 0

From LONDON ROAD STATION—

To LEVENSHULME, HEATON CHAPEL, HEATON NORRIS, and STOCKPORT 9-55, 10-30, 11-20
„ STOCKPORT (only) 10-45, 10-55
„ CREWE 10-55, 11-20
„ CHEADLE HULME, POYNTON, & MACCLESFIELD 10-45
„ STALYBRIDGE, and intermediate Stations..10-0, *11-35
                *Saturdays only.

From OXFORD ROAD STATION—

To ALTRINCHAM and BOWDON, and intermediate Stations 10-0, 10-30, 11- 0
„ BROADHEATH, DUNHAM MASSEY, HEATLEY and WARBURTON, LYMN and WARRINGTON 10-45

From SALFORD—

To RADCLIFFE BRIDGE, BURY, and RAMSBOTTOM.. 11- 0

TRAM-CARS (FROM DEANSGATE).

HIGHER BROUGHTON : Every 10 minutes to 11 o'clock. Saturdays, 10-45 and 11-30, extra.
PATRICROFT (*via* OLDFIELD ROAD AND WEASTE) : 9-30.

PEEL PARK and PENDLETON : Every 7½ minutes to 11-0.
WEASTE (*via* REGENT ROAD) : Every 8 minutes to 11 o'clock. Saturdays, till 11-30.

OMNIBUSES.

ALEXANDRA PARK : Every 5 minutes to 10-30.
BROOKS'S BAR : Every 4 minutes to 11 o'clock.
CHEADLE : 9-5, 10-5.
CHEETHAM HILL : Every 10 minutes to 11 o'clock. Saturdays only, 10-45.
DIDSBURY : 9-30, 9-45, 10.
HARPURHEY and QUEEN'S PARK : Every 7½ minutes to 11. Saturdays only 11-15.
LONGSIGHT : Every 5 minutes to 10-30. 10-40, 10-50, & 11.
LOWER BROUGHTON : 9-0 and 9-30.

MILES PLATTING, &c., and HOLLINWOOD : 9-0, 9-30, 10. Saturdays only 9-15 and 9-45.
OLD TRAFFORD (*via* ALL SAINTS') : Every 15 minutes, from 9 to 10 o'clock.
OLD TRAFFORD (*via* DEANSGATE) : 9-30.
RUSHOLME : Every 15 minutes to 10-25, and 11 o'clock.
SWINTON (per Tram-car to Pendleton) : 9 o'clock. Saturdays, 9-30 and 10.
WITHINGTON : 9-45, 10-30, 10-45.

CAB FARES (FROM ST. PETER'S CHURCH)

	s.	d.
Assize Courts, Strangeways	1	0
Belle Vue Entrance, Hyde Road	2	3
„ Longsight	2	3
Birmingham-street, London Road	1	0
Botanical Gardens, Old Trafford	1	9
Brunswick-street, Ardwick Green	1	0
Bury New Road, Waterloo Road, Cheetham	1	0
Butler-street, Bradford Road	1	3
Butler-street, Oldham-road	1	3
Cavalry Barracks, Barrack-street, Hulme	1	0
Chancery Lane, Ashton Old Road	1	0
Chorlton Road, Stretford Road	1	0
College Road, Whalley Range	2	0
Collyhurst-street, Oldham Road	1	3
Cornbrook (Pomona Gardens)	1	3
Devonshire-street, Hyde-road	1	3

	s.	d.
Dickenson Road, Rusholme	1	0
Eccles Old Road, Bolton Road	2	0
Infantry Barracks, Regent Road	1	9
Lady Barn Lane, Withington	3	6
Leaf Square, Broad-street, Pendleton	1	0
Moss Lane East, Moss Side	1	6
Nelson-street, Upper Brook-street	1	3
Polygon, Clowes-street, Broughton	1	9
Radnor-street, Preston-street, Hulme	1	0
Regent Road, Ordsall Lane, Salford	1	0
Trafford Hotel, Old Trafford	2	0
RAILWAY STATIONS :—		
London Road	1	0
Oxford Road	1	0
Victoria	1	0

Getting Home. Transport arrangements for suburban patrons, Theatre Royal programme, 1881.

VI. PLAYBILLS AND PROGRAMMES

[480] Barnum, P. T., and J. A. Bailey. *Programmes.* Southampton: Walter Hill & Co. Ltd., [n.d.]
Th791.1 Ba11

[481] Birmingham Public Libraries. Reference Department. *Manchester Playbills in Birmingham Reference Library.* 1955. [Typescript]
Th792.094273 Bi1

[482] Evans, John, ed. *Programmes and Bills of Manchester Theatres and Concerts, 1886-94.* 6 vols. 1886-94.
B.R.F792.4273 M41

[483] Harte's Grand Palace and Fairyland, Ashton-under-Lyne. *Playbill. Monday, August 3rd, 1896, and during the week.* Manchester, 1896. [Printed on silk.]
Th792.094273 As1

[484] Jackson, Sir Barry. *Sir Barry Jackson Presents his Company at the Palace Theatre, Manchester for a short season only commencing Monday, May 30th, 1932.* 1932.
Th792.094273 Ja1

[485] Manchester Central Library. *Programme of Entertainments at the Civic Theatre to Celebrate [the] Centenary of Manchester's Charter.* 1938.
M68/21/4

[486] Manchester Youth Theatre. *Playbills, Leaflets, etc.,* 196-.
Th792.094273 Ma238

[487] *Miscellaneous Playbills: Manchester, excluding the major theatres, 1789-1933.* 2 vols.

Vol.1: Albion Hotel, Athenaeum, Bull's Head, Mr. Burn-and's Circuses, Commercial Hotel, The Exchange (various premises in Exchange Street.)

Vol.2: The Folly, Free Trade Hall, Gentlemen's Concert Hall, Lower Mosley Street Schools, premises in King Street, Mechanics' Institution, New Court Room, Royal Olympia Theatre and unidentified places of entertainment, 1789-1933.
Th792.094273 Pl1

[488] *Miscellaneous Provincial Theatre Playbills, excluding Manchester.* 3 vols.

Vol.1: Ashton-under-Lyne, Barton, Blackburn, Bolton, Bury, Buxton, Carlisle, Chester, Chowbent, Dublin, Exeter, Glossop, Hyde, Liverpool, Margate, Mottram.

Vol.2: Oldham, Rochdale, Salford, Southport, Stalybridge, Stockport, Tyldesley, Warrington, Wigan.

Vol.3: (Larger bills) Bolton, Bury, Cowcaddens, Dugles, Fleetwood, Liverpool, Nottingham, Salford, Southport. c.1700-c.1800.
Th792.094273 Pl1

[489] Pan Theatre Company. *Playbills, 1982- .*
ThF792.094273 Pa4

[490] Paramount Theatre, Manchester. *Opening Souvenir [programme].* 1930.
Q792.094273 Pa5

[491] Profundis Theatre Company. *"Operation Grapple" by Peter Quilter.* Leaflet, 1991.
ThQ792.094273 Pr296

[492] Pub Theatre, Manchester. *Handbills and Newsletters.* 1976-. [At the Band on the Wall, Swan Street]
ThF792.094273 Ma267

[493] *Scrapbook of Theatre Programmes, etc., 1905-7.* 1905-7. [Mostly of Manchester and Blackpool theatres.]
Th792.42 S71

[494] Scrapbooks. *A Collection of Cuttings Covering the years 1866-1907.* 1866-1907. 58 vols. [Each volume is partially indexed and collective MS index to the first 50 volumes] (1866-1905). Includes many local theatre programmes and playbills]
WMR780.2 SJ3

[495] *Scrapbooks containing items relating to the theatre.* 7 vols. 1901-15. [Includes much material relating to Manchester theatres]
F792.0942 Sc1

[496] Sladen-Smith, Frank. "The Unnamed Society". *Drama* N.S. No. 13 (1949) 28-31.
792.42 D20

[497] Sutton, Charles William. *Newspaper and other cuttings, with some programmes and other matter relating to the Manchester Stage from early days to the beginning of the 20th century.* 4 vols. [Collection includes R. W. Procter's "Manchester in Holiday Dress" from the *Manchester Guardian,* 1864 and newspaper cuttings, letters, programmes and playbills]
Th792.094273 Ma60

[498] Theatre Union, Manchester. *Prospectus, 1939.* Manchester: Cloister Press Ltd., 1939.
Th792.0942 Th4

[499] *Theatrical Performers, 1906-1952: Newspaper Cuttings Scrapbook*. 1906-52. [Mainly about performers from the Manchester area.]
ThF792.094273 Th571

[500] Thornber, Harry. *The Arts Club, Manchester. Catalogue of engravings of theatrical scenes and portraits*. 1888.
792 M20

Theatre Royal poster advertising Christmas pantomimes, 1881-2.

At the Large Room in the Exchange,
MANCHESTER.
FOR TWO MORE EVENINGS ONLY.
This present WEDNESDAY, and FRIDAY.
December 7th, and 9th,

The Celebrated Shakspearean Hero,

YOUNG ROSCIUS,
MASTER GROSSMITH,
FROM READING, BERKS,
ONLY SEVEN YEARS AND A HALF OLD!

Will give, in this Town, on his way to Scotland, TWO EVENING'S AMUSEMENTS, when he feels confident he will meet with that support he has never failed to receive in London, Birmingham, Liverpool, and all the Cities and Towns he has visited.

PART FIRST.
After a PROLOGUE, written expressly for the purpose,
The INFANT ROSCIUS will give his ADVENTURES in the READING COACH;
WHEN HE WILL IMITATE THE FOLLOWING CHARACTERS: viz.

A Frenchman, and a Fat Lady. An Affected Lady. A Tipsey Politician. A Stage Manager, and two Candidates for the Stage. His own Success.

After which, the INFANT ROSCIUS will go through his much admired and laughable comedy, called

PECKS OF TROUBLES;
OR, THE DISTRESS OF A FRENCH BARBER;
IN WHICH HE WILL PERSONATE THE FOLLOWING CHARACTERS, A-LA-MATTHEWS:

| 1 | 2 | 3 | 4 | 5 | 6 | 7 |

1 Miss Deborah Grundy, 'an old Maid, in love) .... Master GROSSMITH!
2 Spindleshanks, (a dandy fortune hunter .... Master GROSSMITH!!
3 Monsieur Frizeur in a Peck of Troubles about cutting Old Grundy's Face, (with a Song .... Master GROSSMITH!!!
4 Old Grundy, in search of the Frenchman, to give him a receipt in full for his carelesness .... Master GROSSMITH!!!!
5 Betty, the Housemaid, in Love with Corporal Rattle, (with a Song, " Yes, aye, for a Soldier's wife I'll go") .. Master GROSSMITH!!!!!
6 Corporal Rattle, as hot as gunpowder, in love with Betty .... Master GROSSMITH!!!!!!
7 Timothy Clodhopper, a Servant of all work to Old Grundy, bewailing his unfortunate love for Betty, who has run off with Corporal Rattle, (with the laughable Song, " The Washing Tub,") which finishes the Piece ... Master GROSSMITH!!!!!!!

Master GROSSMITH will then Sing his RAGING FAVOURITE, " The FARMER and BETSY BAKER," with many other COMIC SONGS, in the course of the Evening.

SHYLOCK.

PART SECOND.
The FIRST NIGHT will commence with
HAMLET'S SOLILOQUY on LIFE and DEATH.
Hamlet, Prince of Denmark..... Master GROSSMITH.
And on the SECOND and LAST NIGHT, a FAVOURITE SCENE in DOUGLAS.
Douglas........... Master GROSSMITH.
AFTER WHICH, ON EACH NIGHT,
THE TRIAL SCENE IN THE MERCHANT OF VENICE.
Shylock........... Master GROSSMITH.
WITH THE TENT SCENE IN RICHARD THE THIRD.
Richard the Third..... Master GROSSMITH.
The INFANT ROSCIUS will conclude the whole by PERFORMING a PIECE on his

MUSICAL GLASSES.

RICHARD III

DRESS BOXES, 4s.—SECOND BOXES. 3s.—PIT, 2s.
Children under 12 years of age, and Schools over 15 in number, will be admitted at half-price.

N. B. The whole of the WARDROBE, which is very costly and extensive, is got up by Mr. WILLIAM SHAKESPEARE, of the Royal Haymarket Theatre, London The SCENERY adapted for the purpose is Painted by JONES, BILLINGS, and BURTON—the whole of which will be exhibited.
Doors to be opened at half past 7, to commence at 10 minutes past 8 precisely, and to conclude at 10.

TICKETS may be had at T. SOWLER'S, Courier Office ; and at the Large Room in the Exchange, from 2 till 4 on the days of Performance, where places for the Boxes may be taken Where also may be had, a neat Pamphlet, price 6d. dedicated to J. JONES, Esq. Founder of the Royal Cobourg Theatre, London, the Life and Proceedings of the INFANT ROSCIUS, just published by Cowslade and Co. Mercury Office, Reading, Berks, the Birth place of Master Grossmith. [T. SOWLER, PRINTER, COURIER OFFICE.]

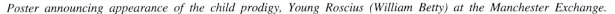

Poster announcing appearance of the child prodigy, Young Roscius (William Betty) at the Manchester Exchange.

VII. PERIODICALS AND ANNUALS

[501] Censor, C. (pseud.) *The Thespian Mirror, or Poetical Strictures; on the professional characters of Mr. Cooke, Mr. Ward, Mrs. Powell, Mr. Bates, Mrs. Taylor, Miss Conerly's, Mr. Banks, Mr. Harding, Mrs. Banks, Mr. Grist, Mr. Richardson, Miss Daniels, Mr. Tyrrell, Mr. Davis, Mrs. Cornely's, Mr. Barrett, Mr. Francis, Mr. Clegg, and Mr. Ryley. Of the Theatres Royal, Manchester, Liverpool and Chester.* Manchester: printed for the Author, 1793.
L347

[502] *Drama.* 1919-1989. London: British Drama League. [1919-39: monthly. 1940-89: quarterly.]
792.42 D20

[503] *The Drama Magazine: the Journal of National Drama.* London: London Drama, 1990-.

[504] *Era Almanack and Annual.* 1868-1918. [48 vols 1868-69 title is *The Era Almanack*; 1870-1913 title is *The Era Alamanack and Annual.*] Library wants 1894 and 1916.
792 E6

[505] *Footlights: a Journal of Theatrical Gossip and Dramatic News.* Vol. 1, no. 2 (20th Jan)- Vol. 1, no. 3 (27th Jun) 1884. [Weekly. The original is only to be consulted in special circumstances: BRF072 D1/5]
MF836/5

[506] Greater Manchester Drama Federation. *Curtain Call: the Journal of the Greater Manchester Drama Federation.* Manchester: The Federation, May 1979-. [Irregular. Ed. by A. Dobson.]
Th792.094273 Cu1

[507] Greater Manchester Drama Federation. *Yearbook and Membership List [no. 1], 1985-.*
ThQR792.094273 Gr1

[508] *Hardacre's Annual, Christmas 1892.* Manchester: The Market Street Press Works, 1892. [Published on behalf of J. Pitt Hardacre, lessee of the Comedy Theatre, Manchester, on the occasion of the pantomime "Mother Goose". Contains contributions by "Nunquam" (Robert Blatchford) and "The Bounder" (E. F. Fay).]
Th792.4273 H4

[509] *Journal of Dramatic Reform.* No. 1 (Jan. 1878)- No. 30 (May 1883). Manchester: Cartwright, Rattray and Co. [Monthly circular of the Dramatic Reform Association.]
792 D40

[510] *Lancashire Figaro and Northern Charivari (Weekly).* Vol. 1, no. 16, (20 Jan. 1881)-vol. 3, no. 87, (25 May 1882). [Comment on local topics, mainly theatrical. Incomplete.]
q052 Ll25

[511] *The Lancashire Magazine; or, Manchester Museum (Weekly).* No. 2. ([Feb?] 1763)- No. 52, (21st February 1764). Manchester, 1763-4. [Subtitle of No. 52 is *Manchester Weekly Amusement.* Each article is paged separately. v. 1. contains "Miscellaneous entertainments" [No. 2. 1-49?]; and "The Chronological History" (issued fortnightly, and later entitled "The History of the Times".) v. 2. contains nos. 2, 10, 12, 15-23, 27-28, 33 and 52. The loose parts are nos. 3, 5, 16, 24-26, 29 and a portion of no. 6. Incomplete]
B.R.052 L121

[512] *Lancashire Stageland, Feb. 1st, 1908.* Vol. 1, no. 1, 1908.
792.0942 La1

[513] *The Looking Glass: a Reflex of the Times.* No. 1 (Dec. 1877)-No. 7 (Jun. 1878) [Monthly. Contains social, satirical, theatrical, musical and artistic articles.]
F052 L136

[514] *Manchester Dramatic and Musical Review.* [14 Nov 1846-4 Sept 1847.] Manchester: Manchester and Salford Advertiser Office, 1846-7.
Th792.094273 Ma3

[515] *Manchester Figaro (weekly)*, 1881.
ThF792.094273 Ma25

[516] *Manchester Dramatic and Musical Review.* No. 1, 14th Nov 1846- No. 43, 4 Sept 1847. Manchester, 1846-7.
R780.5 Me52

[517] *The Manchester Pantomime Annual. A Souvenir of the Pantomimes of 1911-12.* Leeds: Waddingtons Ltd., 1912. [Ed. by B. Roberts]
Th792.3 Ma15

[518] *Manchester Pantomimes' Annual. Containing stories by all the leading artistes at the Royal, Prince's and Queen's Theatres.* Manchester, 1882. [Ed. by H. A. Duffy.]
Th792.0942733 L522/9

[519] *The Manchester Playgoer: a Monthly Review the Stage, Screen and Sport.* Manchester: W. H. Smith, 1925-.
Th792.094273 Ma50

[520] *The Manchester Playgoer (Quarterly).* Manchester: Manchester Playgoers' Club, 1910-14.
ThF792.4273 M1

[521] *Manchester Programme of Entertainments and Pleasure.* 4th January 1897- 26 March 1934. (Weekly). [61 vols]
ThF792.42 M13

[522] Manchester Public Libraries. Arts Library. *Theatre Periodicals (non-current) in M.P.L. in chronological order.* 1975. [Mainly Manchester journals. Typescript.]
ThF792.094273 Ma7

[523] Manchester Repertory Theatre Ltd. *The Manchester Repertory Theatre Magazine, 1934-1938.* 3 vols. Manchester: Cyril H. Clarke & Co. (printers) for the M.R.T., 1934-39. [With News Programme for September 6th 1937.]
Th792.094273 Ma36

[524] *The Manchester Theatrical Censor (Weekly).* Manchester: Beckett & Boyer, 1828. [6 numbers]
Th792.094273 Th1

[525] *Millgate and Playgoer.* Autumn 1905-Spring 1953. 45v. [Variously entitled *Millgate Monthly*, *Millgate*, *Millgate and Playgoer*, *Playgoer and Millgate*, *Playgoer.* Superseded by *Agenda*, June 1953-.]
052 M37

[526] *On Tour: Woodyer's Theatrical Touring Guide.* Vol. 1, No. 1, 11th Aug 1906-Vol. 3, No. 62, 12th Oct 1907.
Th792 O11

[527] *Panto Annual.* Manchester: Lyons & Moffitt, 1895. (1st ed.) [Edited by "Lynx Eye-Junior".]
Th792.094273 Pa1

[528] *The Phoenix; or, Manchester Literary Journal.* 1820. [Incomplete. Ed. by John Bolton Rogerson. The names of some of the writers have been added in MS. Includes dramatic criticisms.]
820.5 P1

[529] *The Playgoers' Club Journal.* (Manchester Playgoers' Club.) Vol. 2, no. 11 (Jan. 1917) – Vol. 14, no. 25 (Sep. 1934).
792.4273 M20

[530] *The Prompter; or Theatrical Investigator.* Manchester: M. Wilson, [Nov 1815-Apr 1816] (2nd ed.)
Th792.4273 P5

[531] *The Prompter Prompted: or, The Theatrical Investigator Dissected* by Jeremy Collier jun. 1816. [5 issues]

[532] *The Selector: a periodical paper, consisting of familiar essays on men, manners and literature (Weekly).* 1816. [Includes theatre criticism]
B.R.052 S11

[533] Society for Theatre Research. *Bulletin.* N.S., No. 1, July 1975-. [Irregular. Previously issued as part of *Theatre Notebook*]
Q792.0942 So13

[534] Society for Theatre Research. *Transactions of the North West Group, Society for Theatre Research.* Vol. 1, No. 1 (Dec. 1951.)
Th792.09427 S1

[535] *The Sphinx: a Journal of Literature, Criticism and Humour.* June 1868-October 1871. 4v. [Ed. by J. H. Nodal. Also contains references to theatre and drama.]
Q052 S58

[536] *Stage and Field: a Herald of Events at the Theatre, Concert Room, Hippodrome, on the Football Field and Cricket Ground, and Guide to all Amusements in Manchester and District (Weekly).* No. 1 (Nov. 28th 1904)-No. 55 (Mar. 12th 1906). Manchester, 1904-6. [Limited access. Incomplete.]
THF792.42 S25

[537] *The Stage Year Book,* 1908-69. London: Carson & Comerford Ltd. [Incorporating *The Stage Provincial Guide*]
792 S3

[538] *Sunday Chronicle Pantomime Annual.* 1913.
792.3 Su1

[539] *The Theatre: a Monthly Review and Magazine.* 1878-1897. [Library has New Series 1-2 (1878-9), N.S. 1-6 (1880-2), N.S. 1-30 (1883-97).
Q792 T9 [Also on microfilm at **MF792.0941 Br1.**]

[540] *Theatre Arts Monthly: the International Magazine of the Theatre.* Vol. 16 (1932)-.
Q792 T11

[541] *Theatre-Craft.* Nos. 2-5 (1919-21). [Quarterly. 4 volumes. This periodical was amalgamated with *English Review* (052 E20) in October 1921]
792 T15

[542] *The Theatre Industry: the Official Organ of the Theatrical Managers' Association.* Vol. 36, Feb. 1958-. [Monthly]
792.05 Th1

[543] *Theatre Notebook.* Vol. 5, no. 1, October-December 1950-. [Quarterly]
792.0942 T1

[544] *Theatre Research.* Vol. 1 (1958-9)-Vol. 14 (1975). [3 issues per year. *Journal of the International Federation for Theatre Research.*] **792.05 Th4**

[545] *Theatre World.* Vol. 32, no. 178 (Nov. 1939) – Vol. 61, no. 491 (Dec. 1965). [Monthly. Incorporating *Play Pictorial* 1902-39. Combined with *Encore* to become *Plays and Players.* **(792.05 Pl1).] F792 P6**

[546] *Theatrical Examiner; or Critical Remarks on the Daily Performances, with the Bills of the Play.* 1829-1830. 5 numbers. **L546/17**

[547] *The Theatrical Times.* Vol. 1 (1846)-Vol. 3 (1848). 3v. in 2. [Weekly. A microfilm copy at **MF792.0941 Br1** includes 1883-4.] **792.42 T2**

[548] *The Vaudevillian.* Manchester: Manchester Music Hall Association, 198-. [Quarterly] **ThF792.7 Va2**

[549] *What's On: the Pioneer Programme of Amusements.* 1898. [Weekly. A guide to entertainments in Manchester.] **ThF792.094273 Wh1**

[550] *What's On? The Manchester Entertainment Guide.* Dec 1946-. [Monthly] **790 W4**

Gerald Kennedy in As You Like It at the New Queen's Theatre, 1916.

INDEX

Numbers in italics are reference numbers in the bibliography (Part III). Numbers in roman refer to page numbers.

ILLUSTRATIONS ACKNOWLEDGEMENT

The illustrations used in this work have been taken chiefly from the Manchester Theatre Collection. Other illustrations have been provided by the Royal Exchange Theatre Company, Chetham's Library and the Manchester Metropolitan University. We are grateful to the librarians in helping us to locate relevant illustrations and for permission to reproduce them. Our thanks to David Rhodes for making his photograph of the Bridgewater Music Hall available to us. We have made every effort to locate the copyright owners of the printed and illustrated material used, wherever information was available to us.